If you always do
What you've always done,
You'll always have (at best)
What you have already

ISBN: 978 1 8381793 9 7

Dedication

I dedicate this book to the 50 million people every year that take the brave step to set up their own business, the 41.5 million who set up a business from scratch, the 5.6 million that purchase a company for the first time, and the 7.2 million that inherit a business through either family, friends or as a gift!

Those who have the traits required NOT to be an employee, but instead take the path less well travelled. The Discipline, Confidence, and Competitive Spirit to keep going. The Open-Mindedness and Creativity to find and exploit a niche. The Passion, People Skills, and Ethics to deliver something that makes a difference in the world.

Successful entrepreneurs want to see what the view is like at the top of the business mountain. Once they see it, they want to go further. I dedicate all my knowledge, experience, research to these pages, and my ongoing support to each one of you in our quest to stand victorious on Success Summit™.

Jay Allen
Chief Scale Sherpa
My TrueNORTH – The Ethical Coaching Company

Table of Contents

Testimonials

ADDAZERO is like having a business coach, in book format. Jay's years of wisdom shine through the pages and keep you focused on the most critical components of building a growing company. Keep it close and refer to it often, as it will become the instructional manual you wish you found years ago.

David Jenyns, Author of SYSTEMology

A meaty BEAST of a book, 1000% Guide to entrepreneurship, is fool proof if you follow it—an exceptionally well written and informative read that I'll be referring back too many times over.

Lisa Haggar, Group HR Director

It doesn't matter whether you are just setting out, a few years in, or an established company. This book needs to be your reference guide. I have advised over 1000 companies during my career yet still found myself learning from the content of this well-written book. It is rare to find all this information so concise in one place.

Peter Collins, CEO - Fast Forward Growth

To call this written knowledge, a 'book' is too much of a narrow view. For entrepreneurs who desire to SCALE their business, they will call this "a bible of their entrepreneurial journey."

Kamlesh Rajput FCCA, Chairman - Sterling Finance Group

I only wish Jay had been around to write this 40 years ago when my husband and I first set up our business.

We've both learnt more from the pages within this book than we have had running our own business for 40 years!

Alice & Mike Arnot, Partners – Pro-print

Throughout these pages are a strong and thoroughly researched 'A-Z of how to build a business' – giving the reader insight into both the pitfalls and mistakes made by many business leaders and how to overcome them.

ADDAZERO is a perfect book for those that are new to business or for the kind of companies that have grown out of an individual or group of people's passions without any formal business training.

Lily Newman, Goldman Sachs Senior Trainer – Morgan James Consulting

From first opening the cover and reading the Foreword, I was hooked and knew this would be one of those books I simply cannot put down.

I am on my fifth attempt to read it from cover to cover now, and still finding there is so much practical guidance here that I'm still putting it down and going to immediately implement the teachings, that my business continues to grow, whilst I am reading the next chapter!

Mark Harris, Senior Partner – Harris & Bucknall Solicitors

If you are SERIOUS about building a significant and sustainable business for both you and your family to benefit from (along with all the team). Then stop whatever else you are doing, and do you, your business, and your future a favour and READ THIS BOOK

Scott Metcalf, Director – Metcalf Associates

Acknowledgements

I have a few special acknowledgements to mention, whom without, this book would simply never have come to be.

Woolworths! – Without having closed your doors for the last time in 2008, the set of circumstances that subsequently unfolded would never have given me the need or desire to commit to this level of research and discovery.

UCLAN University – 2nd & 3rd-year students, who helped make up my research team, gather, analyse and correlate the masses of data we collected to identify the flaws leading to this project taking shape.

Both the **Chamber of Commerce** and **Federation of Small Businesses** – who supported the polling of members to determine the extent of the identified flaws in SME businesses.

The **Explorer Mastermind groups** within My TrueNORTH – Without whom, I would not have sufficient test data to quantify our theoretical assumptions and determine the impact our #ADDAZERO Business Challenge would have on your subsequent SCALE.

My dear friend, **Guy Bartlett** – For demonstrating that from small acorns, great oak trees grow. Your dedication to success and sharing that with others remains an inspiration to us all. My sincerest thanks for such a valued contribution in setting the scene by writing the book's foreword.

My darling wife, **Amanda** – Thank you from the bottom of my heart. Your trust, faith, encouragement, and understanding enable me to be all I am today, tomorrow, and always.

Foreword

When Jay asked me if I would be willing to write a foreword to this book, I was extremely flattered and most happy to do so. Jay Allen is an impressive individual and, if you have read his previous books (*Battlefield2Boardroom* and *Road2Utopia*), you will know he's led a colourful and eventful life. Such a life brings experience, which is a

euphemism for making lots of mistakes and success.

The business of business should intrigue and excite all business owners and entrepreneurs alike. For many years, it has for Jay and me, and this book is a seminal distillation of how successful businesses can succeed and prosper in this competitive world.

Pay attention to "**The 3 Flaws**". One of the most significant lessons I have learned in my 36 years of military service is "fail to plan – plan to fail"! Jay's advice around effective and continuous planning is critical here. Likewise, we both fundamentally believe that people are everything in a business. It does not matter what tangible assets you have on your balance sheet or whether you run a service business, a manufacturing company, provide finance or consult – your most important assets go home every night. As Jay so rightly shares and demonstrates, practical and inspiring leadership in a business is an art that you must learn, nurture, and pay attention to if you want to achieve your business's goals that you rightly dream of.

16

Great leaders also create great vision and culture. They will not tolerate mediocrity (as he eludes to at length with his book *Battlefield2Boardroom*) but will inspire their people to be the best they can be. If you do that, you will own an asset, not a job – a business that can ultimately thrive and succeed without you – and that should be your goal.

Every business owner I have ever met started their business to allow them to have choices – the choice to decide how they spend their time, who with and at a time of their choosing. Yet all too often, they end up owning a job. Read, absorb, and apply Jay's teaching, and you will end up achieving far more than you ever dreamed of and have fun doing it too!

Guy Bartlett is a guest presenter on BBC television and radio for business and Channel Dave's "The Money Pit," the author of "Business Magic," an entrepreneur's guide to acquiring owner-managed companies, and frequent speaker to business groups across the UK.

Guy has built three separate 7-figure businesses from scratch in a wide-ranging business career and acquired numerous Owner Managed Businesses with revenues exceeding £30m. He's been a trusted adviser to many of the UK's top companies, including Sainsbury's, Manchester City FC, the Royal Mail, and JD Sports.

For over three decades, he has enjoyed a parallel career in the British Army and Reserve, serving around the world and decorated for his service. Dynamic, humorous, and straight-talking, he is highly personable and adept at getting the most from people, whether they are business owners, soldiers, Members of the Cabinet, or spinal surgeons!

Preface

This book is by NO MEANS your Sunday afternoon, curl-up-on-the-sofa read! In fact, it could be a book not quite like anything else you have ever read! It has been some four years in the planning. It incorporates well over 150 studies, research points, and 18 months of testing, reviewing, amending, and re-reviewing before it considered valid as worthy of making it to these pages.

Be advised: This book will NOT make you rich. Nor shall it fix every problem or hurdle that you face. There is NO guarantee that anything in your life will suddenly change by reading it, get better, or that any problem will go away. You see, it's a book, not a magic wand!

I CAN assure you that this book has been borne from studying over 150 national and international businesses that have failed. There is so much to learn from failure. And having been significantly affected within my previous company by the collapse of Woolworths in 2008. I set out to understand HOW and WHY businesses can grow to such a size as to become a household name, only to fail?

And the researching findings shocked me!

You see, I found that of the 153 companies we have studied, almost all of them (more than 90%) KNOW there were fundamental flaws within their business. Which, if the business was impacted or affected by specific external influencers (not that uncommon in business: like a recession, or hostile take-over bid, or change in market interest), they were destined to fail! The senior management within each company was more than aware of the flaws. - There was a whole herd of elephants in the corner of each boardroom; nobody was willing to acknowledge or discuss!

This intrigued me...

I wondered at what point in a business's growth do these flaws begin to arise.

How big does a business have to become before these flaws are so significant that they can cause collapse?

At what point does a managing director or other senior decision-maker see them and, rather than address it, choose to bury it and hope it never occurs?

To better understand this, I reached out to two of the largest small business associations in the UK and asked them to question their membership, asking three fundamental questions:

1. *Do you have an up-to-date, written business plan referred to regularly and to which all critical decisions are made?*

2. *Do you have documented systems and processes for each action within the business? Are these determined and tested by your people, rather than created by management/leadership and imposed on the people?*

3. *Do you have a means of measuring the impact of decisions made within each business area (Sales, Marketing, Finance, etc.) and its impact on the other business elements?*

What I learned from the initial research and the data received from this secondary research prompted me to begin working on helping business owners – from SME to PLC – understand more of **The 3 Flaws** and the impact failing to address them has on their businesses.

We wanted to find a means of helping both entrepreneurs and business owners avoid the same ill fate we have witnessed so many times within our research.

Therefore, we listed several questions a business owner would need to satisfy to ensure they did not fall foul of the flaws and put themselves and their business at risk of either going or growing broke. Yes, you read it right, GROWING broke. Poor cash flow management, resulting in profitable companies, STILL failing!

The questions were tested on 12 business owners with whom we had a longstanding working relationship. We worked with each of them for 12 months, asking the questions and implementing actions to find flaws.

As I say, it's taken four years to put this all together and then test this theory by working with business owners to implement the learnings and see the difference it made to both them and their businesses. With the newfound competencies and confidence to act, we quickly began to see business owners of all sized companies were making more rapid progression than they ever had before.

We saw more significant decisions being made quicker and with more confidence and conviction. The results of which, businesses that had until now 'survived' were beginning to thrive.

The momentum continued to gather as the owner-managers noticed the results, and it resulted in 7 of the 10 in our test group becoming National Finalists in the Entrepreneur Awards. But beyond that, it revolutionised them and their businesses. Work was being done quicker, more effectively, and more efficiently. Staff happier and more engaged.
An increase in enquiries was creating more customers, who were spending more money more frequently and

recommending the business to others. Traction was taking hold, and it was a sustaining way beyond our involvement.

ADDAZERO is not a storybook of success, more a reference book of how you can achieve it!

However, for this book to be effective, you can't merely read it. It would be best if you learned to embrace all I share within it and, from that, understand how this relates to you and your business. You need to ACT to see the results. It could be that, following the guidance in this book, you have a stable foundation on which to SCALE. As a result, you may choose to amend and 'upgrade' your ambitions for both you and the business and continue to grow significantly and sustainably. Alternatively, it may be that you confidently grow the company to a size that enables you to sell the business as a going concern and release the equity for you to do whatever it is in life you want to achieve, leaving a legacy for others to continue.

I have already done at least 80% of the hard work in the days, weeks, months, and years of research and testing to establish whether this programme works across online/offline, product/service, new/old, traditional/modern businesses. There remains around 20% left to determine how best to apply the learnings into YOUR business because you and your business are unique to you.

But it will require you to do 80% of the application. As stated at the very beginning, the book will not add a zero to your personal or business finances. Not unless you DO the things I discuss. However, once you have, the business will have a stable foundation, sufficient to grow significantly and sustainably, and add a zero to your Personal Disposable Income.

However, **you are not alone**.

We have created and are growing both a physical and online community of other like-minded entrepreneurs, business owners, and other people with significant control of the business so that collectively we may all learn from the application and benefit from the results.

This book shall start by identifying **the 3 Flaws** found in all the businesses we studied and more than 85% of the micro/SME businesses we surveyed.

Then we shall take a deep dive into each of these, offering practical guidance on how to review, amend, and circumnavigate these flaws so they don't impact you and your business.

And finally, once these processes and practices are in place, we will provide a test and means for you to begin accelerating the speed and direction of growth of your business. You will do this with the competence and confidence to make more significant and more impactful decisions quicker and more succinctly because you have dedicated more time to working concurrently ON the business rather than sequentially IN the business; both you and the business benefit financially.

The 3 Flaws

In researching the key factors that led to businesses and industries' failure in various sectors across the UK, we identified three common flaws across the board. While these are shown in frequency in no order of priority, we found them to be a significant contributory factor in the companies' eventual demise.

Flaw 1 – No Business Plan

There are still too many business owners who appear to think a business plan is only a requirement when applying for funding! And yet, nothing could be further from the truth. I have met multiple business owners, some of them quite sizeable businesses, who would argue, "*I've got this far without one; why do I need to start now?*"

And the simple fact is:

> *Unless you have a business plan, you are still driving blind!*

I do not wish ill of anybody. However, the problem with a plan that's 'in your head' is that it is in YOUR head. And without documenting it and sharing it with others (from whom you may benefit from their input, knowledge, and insight), only you will have the slightest idea as to whether you are heading in the right direction or not. Likewise, by failing to share your knowledge and insight, you are less likely to be approached and hear the wisdom and insight they have to offer.

> *You may well know what you know.*
> *But you don't know what you don't know!*

Finally, while you are 'hands-on' and working 'in' the business, there is nobody in the watchtower navigating the ship!

However, before you tick this off the list thinking, *"I've got one of those,"* my next question would be:

Where is it?

You see, while a small number of businesses' downfall was because they didn't have a structured plan and were merrily free-flowing, hoping they would get to their preferred destination, others did have a plan but still failed.

However, after a little further digging in these cases and soon learned the business plan was significantly out of date or forgotten. It had been carefully mapped out at one stage of the business (probably when it first launched) but had then been filed in a draw marked IMPORTANT, only never to see the light of day again!

A Business plan must be a LIVING document, kept up to date, kept at the front of mind, and all critical business decisions are made.

However, other businesses had a plan that was up to date and yet still failed.

This was the hardest to research, as we needed to understand HOW and WHY. However, the research soon un-earthed that it was not adhered to whilst the business plan was up to date. We found that it was often after the introduction of a new senior hire. Or when there had been an unexpected impact on the business caused by external influence (a change in market preference or a newcomer to the industry with a disruptive influence). That in the moment of panic, the plan had gone to the wall in favour of 'trying something new.'

The conclusion from this research was that the business requires an up-to-date business plan, which is agreed by all within the team as the right way forward and adhered to, modified by mutual consent and not at the expense of the maverick behaviour of one or two individuals.

Flaw 2 – Neglecting People, System, & Process

There are three essential elements in every growing business:

1. People
2. Systems
3. Processes

Our research found that when businesses became under pressure, either internally through extensive, rapid growth or externally by hostile take-over bids or financial turbulence within the market, companies did one of two things:

Those who thrive under pressure are the ones who recognise PEOPLE as the most costly asset to the business and so worked with people to modify, adapt, and overcome Systems and Process issues to support them in their roles. People came first, training budgets were not affected, and investment in staff welfare was maintained. In return, employees pulled together, and they did more than they were either salaried or expected to do.

Whereas, there was a difference in businesses where the pressures became more evident, and they moved to RULE. They insisted employees stringently followed the processes and systems in place. They failed to acknowledge creativity and engagement and only saw humans as a resource. The people were unable to bond further as a team, and this segregation caused fractures. People began working 'to rule,' and the business lost its focus, edge, and implode.

> *The GREATEST investment any business can make*
> *is in the training & development of its people.*

Get it right, and they will reward you and the business for years to come. Get it wrong, and they can easily cost you every penny the company ever made.

Flaw 3 – Ignoring the Holistic Business

The most complex of the flaws we discovered was what I refer to as ignoring the holistic business. Just as in Newton's third law of motion, there is an equal and opposite reaction for every action. And this is so for every aspect of the business: its energy, focus, and effort.

The eight elements we identified in every successful SCALE business:

1. Clarity in the *Mindset & Motivation* of the business owner(s)
2. A well-defined Business *Vision, Values, Culture & Purpose* the stakeholder(s) wish to achieve for the business.
3. A Business **Strategy and Structure** are relevant to achieving the outcomes.
4. The *Marketing Management* required to achieve this.
5. A proven *Sales Strategy* and negotiation capability to determine profitable "WIN, WIN, WIN" outcomes.
6. Full and faultless *Money/Margin Management* that is embedded throughout the business.
7. Benchmarking of **Service & Delivery** sufficient to build FANS not just customers.
8. A *Winning Team* that buys into all the aforementioned.

To download infographic: **www.addazero.co.uk/infographic**

Everything is linked. If you haven't got everything in place, working well, and understanding its impact, it's like driving a car low on oil. It may start, it may go, but one day it will seize!

There must be an understanding of each action's impact on EVERY other business element so that one aspect is not thriving at the expense of another part's demise.

We spent a long time looking at these elements and their impact on each other and concluded that there are eight elements to every business: online or offline, product or service. At one level or another, all of these are present. The eight segments have subsequently become the eight chapters within this book.

Each of the eight elements must be managed and maintained for your business to enable sustainable scale.

Businesses that thrive (and continue to do so) are the ones who understand and nurture the relationship between these segments and ensure they work as a whole. Businesses that struggle (and ultimately fail) are the ones in which silos become apparent, where one 'department' fails to see the other departments as customers/suppliers to them. This approach breeds either competitor or contempt culture, either of which strangles engagement and leads to downfall.

In recognising these three business flaws, it has been possible to identify and list the eight essential elements that each business must consider to become successful and determine the impact each has on subsequent success.

The remainder of this book will take you through each of these eight elements in more detail and in turn.

However, before we delve any further, I would like to point out…

THIS ENTIRE PROCESS STARTS AND ENDS WITH YOU!

You see, it does not matter whether you quit your job, got made redundant, or retired. Or if you started your business when you were still at prep, juniors, high school, or college. It does not matter how much knowledge, background, or experience you have or do not have. Or whether you are going to trade online/offline, with a product or service-based business providing Business to Business (B2B) or Business to Consumer (B2C). It does not matter what sector you are in. If you are going to succeed, it must come from YOU.

Whether you have set up your own business, an inherited family business, or bought an existing business, it all started with someone, somewhere deciding to start a business. As a business owner, entrepreneur, or person with significant control of a company, YOU have to have clarity on YOUR vision, YOUR culture, YOUR values, and YOUR purpose BEFORE you can even begin to set the vision for your business.

Please understand, it may well be that you do not currently have any intention to SCALE your business (and that's more than OK.) This book will take you to a place where you will grow and reach a place where you are more than happy. It will also prepare you and the business to scale if you subsequently want to take that next step.

I recall, when I first learnt to swim, all I wanted to achieve was to be safe in the water, to be able to swim to the side, if I ever fell in! Once I reached that, I set a new goal of swimming my first length. Quickly one length became 10, and 10 became 100. As my competence and confidence grew, so did my aspirations. I wanted to learn to dive, to swim faster, further, more efficiently.

Therefore, while we may use GROWTH and SCALE's terminology, think of it merely as a means of aiding your progression to whatever it is you are seeking to achieve.

It may well be that you are keen to learn how to move from a five-figure business to a six-figure company or from multiple six-figure companies to seven. And that you have no plans or goals to SCALE - This book can **certainly** help you to achieve that.

However, it may be that having reached multiple six or seven figures. You begin to wonder what a multiple seven- or even eight-figure business might look like – and by implementing all the teachings within this book, you will have the necessary foundations to achieve this if that is what you decide to do. (As once you can 'tick' everything off the list, you will be ready for the book's sequel: #ADDAZERO – Scale & Exit)

When working with business owners, we have often found their initial aspirations (for them and their business) are far less than they or their business can achieve. It is simply because we don't know what we don't know. We can't imagine being the next Bill Gates, Steve Jobbs, or Elon Musk, so we don't set our heights that high.

However, by applying the teachings in this book and thereby achieving more than they would otherwise have thought capable (especially within the timeframe it can take), it starts to open the mind to what else is possible. And this is where the magic begins...

To transition from growth to SCALE, it will take more from you – at least while you are following this process or transitioning into it – more work, more consideration, more determination. And that means YOU must be clear about what YOU want from this process, beyond a significant and sustainable business.

Is it to buy your forever dream home, a holiday home, or travel around the world?

Is it to take the business regionally, nationally, or internationally? To become the name within your industry/sector?

Is it for the business to continue to grow without requiring you to remain within it – receiving an income without the endless hours?

Or maybe it is something else?

Only once you have clarity on what you want and why can you return to the business to establish whether the business vision, values, and goals align with your own.

It does not matter how young or old you are or how much money you have within your bank balance. There are 60 minutes in an hour, 24 hours in a day, and seven days in a week! While many things are hugely important to us, we must accept that we cannot spend more than 168 hours a week on them – it is a physical impossibility! Therefore, the investment (both in terms of time, consideration, physical and mental energy, sacrifice, and financial) we put into the business has to give us a positive reward. Or one day, we will stop doing it as well, and eventually stop doing it at all!

Clarity of what YOU want is critical before working on the business and your role and responsibilities.

To help, I have posed a series of questions you may want to consider before reading any further...

Ask yourself:

1. What does SUCCESS look like for you,
   your family, your business?
   1.1. Where will you be living?
   1.2. What does a 'typical' day look like?
   1.3. What type/style of clothes do you wear?
   1.4. What car(s) do you drive?
   1.5. Where do you holiday? And how often?
   1.6. How much income do you require to sustain this
        comfortably and without compromise?
2. By when do you want to achieve this?

This list is by no means definitive and requires much consideration. It should be written in the current mindset, uncertain whether it is possible, but in the future, a reflective perspective of having already achieved it!

"What would you do if you knew you couldn't fail? "
Robert H. Schuller

Chapter One:

Mindset & Motivation

Your Business WHY?

If you have ever spent time around kids, you have been subjected to a barrage of the most classic of childhood queries: "Why?"

Even from a young age, we know intuitively that the motive behind an action is the essential piece of any story. When it comes to your business – whether you've already launched or whether you're still in the whiteboard phase– knowing your "why" will help you stay committed to your dream and help others get on board too.

"He who has a why can endure any how."
Frederick Nietzsche

The right reasons

There are many reasons why people become entrepreneurs: personal satisfaction, creative independence, or financial autonomy – the list goes on. Yet all of these have one thing in common. At the core, they all are about freedom.

That freedom can come in many different forms: the freedom to make changes without waiting for corporate green lights, the freedom to offer a product or service that does business differently, or maybe the literal freedom to make that dentist appointment once and for all.

What is it that drives you? The reason probably isn't money– at least it shouldn't be. There is a reason that career counsellors across the country ask the same time-old question: "If money were no object, what would you do?"

Money isn't enough

The siren call for many entrepreneurs is not money; it's freedom. The freedom to chart your own path, the freedom to build what you want with the people you love.

As the owner of your company, you can set your own targets and standards. And while the freedom of not having anyone standing in your way can be invigorating, the stress of knowing there is no one to blame for any failures can be too much to bear. This is when your "why" becomes imperative.

If you are not 100 per cent committed to making your vision a reality, you will not be impassioned enough to nurture your business through its inevitable growing pains.

Businesses rarely make money right off the bat, so the dream of money alone will not be reason enough to see it through. Do not trade in the shackles of your corporate day job for a gilded cubicle of your own making.

If a paycheck is just a means to end, how do you know when you have reached it? Is it after five years? Ten? Or when you finally make a down payment on a house? The more material possessions you acquire – a car, a house, that villa in the south of France – the more that regular, safe paycheck becomes a crutch. So, ask yourself, "Why am I doing this?"

Once you find an answer that speaks to your soul, the next question should be, "What am I waiting for?"

Find your story

You can only become truly accomplished at something you love. Do not make money your goal. Instead, pursue the things you love doing and then do them so well that people cannot take their eyes off you.

The great thing about passion is that it's infectious. And a great story does not have to be dramatic, just genuine.

With so many social marketing campaigns around, customers want to feel like they are supporting a cause, not just buying a product. If your audience knows that you love what you do, not only will they be more confident that you have made the best possible product, but they'll also want to support your enthusiasm by giving you, their business.

Your story is also your link to your core principles. If you set out to make a product with all-natural ingredients, keep that in mind as your business begins to grow. Do not compromise your product's integrity, or you will undermine your customer's trust and everything you have accomplished.

Not every passion is a potential business, and that is OK.

Perhaps you love yoga, and your friends are always saying you should become an instructor. That is great if you enjoy the idea of teaching others. But if the reason you like yoga is that it allows you a quiet escape from the rest of the world, then there is nothing wrong with keeping it all to yourself.

> *"There is no passion for being found playing small,*
> *in settling for a life that is less than*
> *the one you are capable of living."*
> **Nelson Mandela.**

Not sure what your passion is?

Do some market research. Poll your closest friends and family (only people you trust to give you an honest answer) and ask them what they think your strengths are. Not only can it be a huge confidence booster to hear how wonderful they think you are, but they may come up with skills you didn't even realise you had.

Another thing is to ask yourself what sorts of things people ask you for help. Does your tech-savvy make you the first-person people call when they are thinking of buying a new computer?

Do you frequently help family members to write letters or improve their résumés? Maybe you are the best at finding great airline deals, or your broad perspective means people consult your opinion before making a big financial decision.

Whatever it is, think about those things you do for free and extrapolate these skills to see where a potential business could be born.

Passion is contagious

When your enthusiasm is palpable, people want a ticket on your happy train. The key to harnessing that passion is understanding your "why." Why are you passionate about windsurfing? Is it because it helped you lose 30 lbs, get off all your medications, and have a new lease on life?

That is your "why," which is the story you need to share with your customers. You deserve a life you love, so get going and dream on.

Now it is time to deal with each of the eight elements of a business that you need to have in place to significantly and sustainably scaling your business to Success Summit.

Do you have a Business Mindset?

To build the right business infrastructure, you must think strategically, starting with a business mindset.

Here are seven ways of building a positive business mindset.

1. *Knowing that the purpose of business is to make money. Sometimes your hobby is just a hobby. Either you will have a hobby that makes you a little extra cash, or you are going to have a business that requires a higher level of development to acquire a higher level of income.*

2. *Thinking for yourself vs letting other people think for you. Do not allow the experts to control your destiny or dreams; let them help you get there. Take some time to think, document, and research your idea before asking for help. You will be better equipped to ask for exactly what you want and getting it if you do.*

3. *Being more strategic about your business activity. Do not just go to any networking event or take on any job; know what results you want before investing in business activity.*

    3.1.1. *For example, do you know how much it costs you to attend a training session or a networking event - money, family, time, babysitter, petrol, etc.? To recoup your investment, your reasons for investing in*

> *the training must be things other than meeting people and "I just want to learn something."*
>
> 3.1.2. *That's a given when you go to networking (meet people) or training (learn something). Your purpose for attending any event must be one, aligned with your vision, and two, focused on profitability. Make sure you have a specific outcome in mind before investing in business activities like networking and training.*

4. *Knowing that we need to connect with our businesses and that connection is... passion and motivation to achieve. How do you connect with this? By building something, you love that you know others will love also. Finding a problem in the universe that you can solve, and others either have that problem or a desire to see it resolved. And at the same time, you know your profit margin, cash flow, competitive advantage, sales goals, and key profit indicators.*

5. *Understanding strategy and implementing it into your business practices. These days we tend to focus on the day-to-day mundane tasks and deadlines, solving short-term problems, and implementing marketing tactics that are not a good fit for our businesses. Strategy concerns itself with what is ahead, looking at where you are going and how to get there. Thereby making you ask the question: "Is this task in line with where the company is going and/or where I want it to go?"*

6. *Being open to multiple streams of income and numerous businesses. I met a lady at a conference a while back, and I will never forget what she told me: "I have one business that's my passion that makes me a good income, and I run it. I have another business that generates substantial profit for me, and I have someone else to run it." The point: you don't have to put all your eggs in one basket – that's part of having a business mindset.*

7. *Understanding your emotional ties to your business.*
   Understanding your business's emotional ties will allow you
   to break through the barriers that prevent you from doing
   what you say you're going to do and doing what you want to
   do. The next time you get emotional in your business, jot
   down what you feel and what triggered it. This is how you
   begin to recognise which emotions are keeping you from
   doing profitable business.

Every business decision you make today affects your business today, tomorrow, and in the future, so it is essential to become a good strategist. A good strategist looks at all facets of their business today regarding where they are trying to go. A good strategist reacts to problems positively instead of negatively. A good strategist also welcomes change and turns it into an opportunity. A good strategist can respond quickly to the unexpected.

So that is the mindset bit covered, but how about motivation?

What is your motivation strategy?

Often, when entrepreneurs make the bold leap from an employee of a corporation to the leader of their own business, one of the first challenges they face is no longer having a person or group of people above them to set goals, deadlines, and incentives. The responsibility of inspiration becomes a task of self-motivation.

This can be a challenge for many, especially when the experience is new. And the entrepreneur is consumed with working in the business rather than working on it. Any lack of self-discipline and organisation can also affect personal development and family, which are often the first to be put on the back burner.

So, how does an entrepreneur maintain a focus on the business while also staying motivated to become a better person and business leader? The answer is simple: It requires time, dedication, and practice – just as you would expect from a business.

Ten ways to get yourself motivated and working toward your business and personal goals:

1. Set a personal mission statement.

Every business has or should have a vision and mission statement. An idea of what you want to achieve and a mission as to how you know you will have achieved it. Something that describes the organisation's broader goals, culture, and underlying core values.

It is primarily used to set the direction of the organisation and motivate stakeholders. For the same reasons, every entrepreneur should develop his or her own mission statement.

The important thing here is to write down your mission statement, carry it with you, read it aloud, memorise it and tattoo it on your forearm (the latter for the extreme entrepreneurs only). It should serve as a constant reminder of your purpose for becoming an entrepreneur.

2. Make a plan.

Just as in business, a mission statement is useless without a plan to execute it. You should develop and write down your personal and professional plan, including short-term and long-term goals. This plan will not and should not be penned and framed, as it is organic and will change as your personal and professional circumstances change.
The purpose here is to clearly understand what you want to accomplish personally and how you will achieve it.

3. Start with a routine.

Getting yourself motivated is about getting started. For this reason, you should start every day with a great morning routine, which will help your mind and body to be alert, focused, and prepared to create new habits. As part of your routine every morning, you should spend time reviewing and refining your plan.

4. Set aside time for yourself.

Because entrepreneurs can often get completely caught up in their business, it is important to set personal time during the day for yourself. During this time, allow yourself the flexibility to take a walk, think and meditate or even exercise. Also, learn to leverage this time to eat properly and drink water, two crucial habits that will go a long way to helping you stay focused.

5. Plan ahead and set reminders.

Even with a plan, it can be challenging to stay in a routine. For this reason, develop a habit of setting reminders throughout the day for your important tasks and daily goals. Use your alarm, with a manageable volume, to remind yourself to stay focused on the job. An alarm that says, "Get off Facebook and back to work" would be perfect for some of us!

You can also stay on track using time blocking or the process of setting specific durations of time in your calendar for particular work, projects, or tasks. Need a little more help? Consider these unconventional motivational and productivity apps for the hardcore entrepreneur.

6. Set rewards.

We are naturally wired to react to incentives, so be prepared to reward yourself for accomplishing a goal or maintaining a habit. Just like in business, you should recognise and reward small victories along the way to long-term, broader goals.

And, if you need more incentive, consider a clock that counts down your remaining life and reminds you to make the best of what time you have left.

7. Engage friends.

Sometimes the best motivation comes from peer pressure. Engage your friends and colleagues to help motivate you both toward individual and shared goals. Consider mobile apps that make the engagement fun, such as Make Me, ChallengedApp, KlashApp, or simply text your challenge to your partner.

8. Indulge in inspirational activities.

Sometimes, you just need to look outside your circle for motivation. When this happens, re-watch a movie that you found inspiring. During your lunch break, watch a TED talk. Or listen to an inspirational podcast during your commute, on your daily walk, or while you are enjoying your personal time alone.

9. Stay positive.

There is no one-size-fits-all answer to what makes people happy, with definitions, theories, and opinions abound. For me, I have a simple mantra that I turn to when I need a boost. It is merely *"Choose happy."*

By saying that phrase and mustering up an authentic smile, I find my mood and motivation is elevated exponentially.

If you find yourself weighed down by the people around you or are frequently the most intelligent person in the room, you are probably in the wrong place. My most significant motivation sources are the passionate, hardworking people around me who have grand dreams and brilliant minds. Build your team and your community with people who push you to grow and think outside the box. When you know you must be on your toes to keep up, you will work harder and think bigger. That same passion will ignite in you.

Thoughts are powerful, and negative thoughts can prevent you from achieving your goals. The flip side is that positive thoughts can be just as powerful. The next time you feel unmotivated, simply visit www.addazero.co.uk and download our 50 positive thoughts to re-energise yourself. Really: They work!

The power of positive thinking is not just an adage – it is scientifically proven that positive thoughts (and the elimination of negative self-talk) can improve your mood, feelings, and performance. These thoughts should get you started doing whatever it is you need the motivation to do. The rest is up to you.

10. Sleep

Finally, never underestimate the value of a good night's sleep for personal motivation. After years of experience and self-experimenting, I have found that, with few exceptions, no unfinished task or missed goal is worth the misery that comes with losing sleep over it.
More importantly, with a fresh night of rest, these tasks and goals become infinitely easier to finish the following day.

In my years as an entrepreneur, author, and business advisor, I have seen others fail and have had countless failures of my own. I have stayed up endless late nights working on a new project, only to rip it apart and start all over again. I have heard *"no"* more times than I can count.

But through all the trials and tribulations of being my own boss, I have learned one crucial lesson: staying motivated is a daily choice.

Though difficult, your success depends on training your mind to see the excitement and good in your daily work. Focusing on the negative causes of stress, anger, and worry that wear you down mentally and physically with dire consequences: heart disease, chronic anxiety, and heated outbursts with your friends and family.

When you see the excitement and the mundane positivity, you recognise you have a life you can be proud of. Then you are excited to attack!

Knowing yourself

One of my favourite quotes from George Addair is:

> *"Everything you've ever wanted*
> *is on the other side of fear."*

And yet, because so many are fearful of change, afraid of the unknown, fearful of failure (or success), they never approach the line, push through to the other side, and realise all they are capable of achieving.

I have bad news for those who don't like change: The ONLY constant in life is change!

We all must learn to accept that change is constant, so rather than fighting it, it is far better to go with it and see where it takes us. Once we have accepted this, we can then begin to challenge where it takes us and steer our own course.

I am exceptionally fortunate in this regard, having chosen to join the British Army. There is a beautiful (if not a little perturbing) quote from the book of Army discipline taken from Queen Victoria the First Reign – "the purpose of initial (basic) training, is simply to Breaketh the boy, to maketh the man."

However, having experienced basic training in the early 1990s, there was very much two 'halves' to the training. Initially, it was to break you down and challenge your perceptions of what you **thought** you were capable of. And quickly followed by helping to show you what you were **actually** capable of.

Although I no longer wear the uniform, I still apply the same logic to my surroundings, rather than looking at anything as a hurdle and dissuading from approaching it.

I immediately switch back to the soldier within me and break the problem down into every possible scenario to find a means of overcoming the hurdle and turning it into an achievement.

Many, if not all, the ancient martial art disciplines are not about either self-defence or outward violence but are about self-discipline and self-mastery. In the same way, to know anything of others, we must first learn to know ourselves.

Psychometric profiles

One of the easiest and yet most revealing way to get to know yourself is by conducting a psychometric profile.

What are psychometric tests?
Psychometric tests are a standard and scientific method to measure an individual's mental capabilities and behavioural style. They are designed to measure candidates' suitability for a role based on the required personality characteristics and aptitude (or cognitive abilities). They identify the extent to which the personality and cognitive abilities match those required to perform the role. Employers can use psychometric test information to identify the hidden aspects of candidates that are difficult to extract from a face-to-face interview.

Some believe that the psychometric test is not a good measure to assess their natural abilities, personality traits, and suitability for the job. However, psychometric tests are statistically examined and are constructed to be objective and unbiased.

This is done using standard assessment methods to present the same questions and instructions for completing them. Our experience shows that psychometric tests are very reliable in predicting performance, and in most cases, the test report provides an accurate evaluation of the person being tested.

A Brief History of Psychometric Tests
Psychometric tests are by no means a new concept; they have been used since the early twentieth century when used initially only for educational psychology purposes. It was in 1905 that Alfred Binet introduced the first 'intelligence test.'

They have since evolved to become a common feature of the selection process, particularly within large, competitive organisations, which prefer these types of tests to assess each candidate on their acquired skills rather than educational background.

Why and When Are Psychometric Tests Used?
Recruiters like to use psychometric tests for the following reasons:

- ✓ They are objective and impersonal, allowing candidates to be compared in ability terms without unconscious bias.
- ✓ They help to make the recruitment process more efficient and can represent substantial HR costs.
- ✓ They are proven to be reliable indicators of future job performance.

The tests may appear at any stage in the recruitment process, but usually, you will undertake the test at one of these three stages:

- ✓ Immediately after you submit your application form
- ✓ As an add-on to your interview
- ✓ Immediately before or after your actual interview

What do Psychometric Tests Measure?
The term 'psychometric' is coined from the Greek words for mental and measurement. The tests explore three main areas: your capabilities, aptitude for the job, and determining whether

your personality fits in with the vision of the organisation you are hoping to join.

Essentially, the tests are looking to evaluate your intelligence, aptitude, and personality, as well as how you handle pressure and your working style.

What are the Different Types of Psychometric Test?
There are essentially three categories: aptitude tests, skills tests, and personality tests. Let us examine each in turn.

Aptitude Tests
Aim to assess a specific or general set of skills, though this often depends on the type of job that you are applying for.

Categories found within this group include:

Numerical reasoning test
Used to identify how you interpret data, often via a combination of written and statistical information presented in reports, graphs, or charts. This can also be used to assess the necessary mathematical abilities.

Verbal reasoning test
Used to determine your ability to evaluate detailed written information to make an informed decision.

Inductive reasoning test
These require you to identify trends or patterns, typically using diagrammatic information.

Diagrammatic reasoning test
These assess your capacity for logical reasoning using flowcharts and diagrams.

Logical reasoning test
Aims to evaluate your skills in concluding. You may be provided with some information and then asked to decide what you have

been provided with. As such, these tests are also often known as deductive reasoning tests.

Error checking test
Assesses your ability to quickly identify any errors in complex data sets such as codes or combinations of alphanumeric characters.

The job type and sector will determine the type of test that you will have to undertake. For example, inductive or logical reasoning assessments evaluate candidates applying for jobs in science, IT, or other roles where advanced technical skills may be needed.

These tests usually comprise of multiple-choice questions and a specified time frame in which to complete them.

Inductive testing can identify new solutions and strategies to solve the issue, so these tests are used in many firms specialising in technological innovation.

As with any recruitment related test, it is always recommended that you familiarise yourself with the process to know what to expect and are adequately prepared.

Psychometric tests are pretty formal and impersonal, but there are many ways in which you can practice and prepare.

Skills Tests
Skills tests represent a way for employers to evaluate how quickly you can learn a new skill to carry out the job you are applying for competently.

Both capability and skills tests are assessed through paper-based exercises consisting of multiple-choice questions completed under exam conditions.

Increasingly, psychometric tests are completed online using specialist systems that remove the requirement for a paper-based test.

Personality Tests
Personality assessments enable employers to evaluate your suitability based on your behaviour and how you approach your work.

This will be used to determine how well you will fit into the organisation and its culture. Your responses will often be cross-referenced with those of a top-performing employee or successful manager, which will indicate whether you share the same characteristics.

Employers look at many factors during the recruitment process, from your knowledge and experience to your aptitude in decision-making and teamwork.

They will increasingly use personality tests to determine if you have the right attitude and personality to fit in with the company's culture and vision.

Myers Briggs is one of the most used personality tests. After progressing through a series of questions about how you would feel or act in each scenario, you will be assigned to one of sixteen personality types based on your responses.

Employers then review this personality type to see if you would fit in with their organisational values.

There is rarely a time limit, as they are looking for you to answer the questions honestly (though it's worth having a sense of the job description and the employer needs in the back of your head as you go along).

Goal setting

We all know the phrase *"If we always do what we have always done, you will always have (at best) what you have already,"* and yet too many business owners say a year in and year out – next year will be different.

If we want different outcomes, it comes from taking other actions, starting with having different thoughts. Therefore, set your business and yourself a set of STRETCH goals for the next 12 months. Before you set the company up, go back to re-invigorate that inner child within you, the one with drive and passion and absolute impregnability who was invincible and ready to take on the world. NOW sit and write YOUR goals first and THEN the businesses.

Why You Should Be Writing Down Your Goals

We hear a lot about goal setting importance, but most of us don't have clear and measurable goals to work toward. But how important are goals and, if they are vital, how can we make the most effective?

According to a study done by Gail Matthews at Dominican University, those who wrote down their goals accomplished significantly more than those who did not write down their goals. Who does not want to accomplish significantly more? (Feinstein, 2014)

Goal setting steps

Here are four steps to creating clear and measurable goals that will lead you to massive success.

1.   Create a Vision

The first step to creating a goal is to figure out what you want. If you do not know what you want, you don't see what you need to achieve to get there. This is the fun part. You get to dream. What do you want to create for yourself? What does your ideal life look like? Do not be afraid to think big. Take fifteen minutes and document your vision. Take note of the details. What does your day look like? Where are you living? Try to incorporate all senses in your vision to make it most effective. What do you see, hear, smell, taste, and feel throughout this perfect day?

2. Make it Measurable

Take your vision and turn it into a written list of concrete goals. If you are working for yourself in your ideal world, one of your dreams might to start your own company. Choose an achievable time frame to accomplish your goals and measurable details so you know exactly when you have achieved them. What exactly does it mean to start your own company? Make sure to set yourself up for success by creating realistic and achievable goals in the given timeframe.

3. Set Benchmarks

Most of our goals are a build-up of small achievements, sometimes even years of many small successes. Break your goals into small actionable steps and assign realistic time frames to each. Continue to break significant steps into smaller and smaller steps until goals seem less daunting and achievable. Benchmarks are a great way to keep you on track. You may find you are moving more quickly or slowly than you expected. That's not a problem; you can adjust! Fine-tune your expectations and timeline as you gather more information while achieving your benchmarks.

4. Celebrate Your Success

I believe the most crucial part of goal setting is celebrating our successes. How will you reward yourself for hitting your benchmarks along the way? How will you celebrate once you have reached your goal? As you journey towards the realisation of your goals, it is essential to remember your vision. Knowing why we want something can provide us with the motivation and determination to continue to work toward it even when things don't go as planned or are more complicated than we anticipated.

From now on, choose to be among the most successful people and write down your goals. Create a vision for what you want, turn that into a list of measurable goals, set benchmarks, and celebrate your successes along the way.

How to Write Personal Goals

A goal is a way of representing a specific, measurable accomplishment that you want to achieve through effort. A goal may be based on a dream or hope, but a goal is quantifiable, unlike those. With a well-written goal, you will know what you want to achieve and how you will achieve it. Writing personal goals can be both gratifying and incredibly useful. Research has shown that setting goals make you feel more confident and hopeful – even if the goals are not immediately achieved.

As the Chinese philosopher Lao Tzu once said:

> *"A journey of a thousand miles*
> *begins with a single step."*

You can take that first step on your journey of achievement by setting realistic personal goals.

12 Step Guide to writing meaningful Personal Goals

1. Think about what is meaningful to you

Research shows that when you base your goals on something that motivates you, you are more likely to achieve them. Identify areas of your life that you would like to change. At this stage, it's okay for these areas to be pretty broad. Common goals include self-improvement, improving your relationships, or achieving some measure of success with an undertaking, such as work or education. Other areas you could examine might include spirituality, finance, your community, and health. Consider asking yourself some big questions, such as *"How do I want to grow?"* or *"What do I want to offer the world?"* These can help you determine what is most valuable to you. For example, you might think about meaningful changes you would like to see in health and personal relationships. Write those two areas down, as well as what changes you would like to see.

It is okay if your changes are broad at this point. For example, for health, you might write *"improve fitness"* or *"eat healthily."* For personal relationships, you might write *"spend more time with family"* or *"meet new people."* For self-improvement, you might write, *"learn to speak more proficiently or to become a better networker."*

It is not so much about what you choose to do, but that you spend time reviewing what you could be better at and make it a goal and set about improving it!

2. Identify your "best possible self."

Research suggests that identifying your *"best possible self"* can help you feel more positive and happier in life. It can also help you in thinking about what goals are meaningful to you. Finding your *"best possible self"* requires two steps: visualising yourself in the future, achieving your goals, and considering the characteristics, you will need to get you to that place.

Imagine a time in the future where you are your best version of yourself. What would that look like? What would be most meaningful to you? (It's important to focus on what's meaningful to you, rather than on what you may feel pressured to achieve by others.)

Imagine the details of this future self. Think positively. Imagine something that is a *"life dream,"* a milestone accomplishment, or other significant achievements. For example, if your best possible self is a baker with her successful cake bakery, imagine what that looks like. Where is it? What does it look like? How many employees do you have? What type of employer are you? How much do you work?

Write down the details of this visualisation. Imagine what characteristics your *"best possible self"* is using to achieve his/her success. For example, if you are running your own bakery, you need to know how to bake, manage money, network with people, problem-solve, be creative, and determine the demand for baked goods. Write down as many characteristics and skills as you can think of.

Think about which of these characteristics you already have. Be honest with yourself, not judgmental. Then, think about which characteristics you can develop.

Imagine ways for you to build these characteristics and skills. For example, if you want to own a bakery but don't know anything about running a small business. Taking some classes in business or money management would help develop that skill.

3.   Prioritize these areas

Once you have got down a list of areas you would like to see change, you will need to prioritize them. Trying to focus on improving everything all at once could end up feeling overwhelming, and you are far less likely to pursue your goals if you think that they cannot be achieved.

Split your goals into three sections: overall goals, second tier, and third tier. The overall goals are the most important, the ones that come to you most naturally. The second and third-tier are important goals, but they are not as important to you as the overall goals, and they tend to be more specific.

For Example:

Overall:

    1.1. Prioritise health (most important)
    1.2. improve family relationships (most important)
    1.3. take a trip abroad.

2. **Second-tier**:
    2.1. Be a good friend
    2.2. keep the house clean
    2.3. climb Mt. Everest

3. **Third tier**:
    3.1.   Learn to swim
    3.2.   become more efficient at work
    3.3.   exercise every day.

4. **Start narrowing down**

Once you have found the areas you want to change and what changes you would generally like to see, you can begin to distinguish the specifics of what you want to accomplish. These specifics will be the basis for your goals. Asking yourself some questions will answer the who, what, when, where, how, and why of your achievement.

Research suggests that setting a specific goal not only makes you more likely to achieve it. It makes you more likely to feel happier overall.

5. **Determine the Who**

It is important when setting goals to know who is responsible for achieving each part of the goal.
Since these are personal goals, you will probably be the most reliable. However, some goals – such as "spend more time

with family" require others' cooperation, so it's a good idea to identify who will be responsible for which parts.

For example, "learn to cook" would be a personal goal that probably involves only you; however, your goal is to "throw a dinner party," which requires responsibility from others.

6. Determine the What

This question helps determine the goal, details, and results you wish to see. For example, "learn to cook" is too broad to be manageable – it lacks focus.

Think about the details of what you really want to accomplish. "Learn to cook an Italian dinner for my friends" is more specific. "Learn to cook chicken Yakisoba for my friends" is more precise still.

The more detailed you make this element, the more precise the steps you need to accomplish.

7. Determine the When

One key to setting goals is breaking them up into stages. Knowing when specific parts of your plan must be achieved helps you keep on track and gives you a sense of progress. Keep your steps realistic. *"Lose ten pounds"* is unlikely to happen in a matter of weeks. Think about how much time it will realistically take you to achieve each stage of your plan.

For example, *"Learn to cook chicken yakisoba for my friends by tomorrow"* is probably unrealistic. This goal could cause you much stress because you try to achieve something without giving yourself enough time to learn (and make the inevitable mistakes).

"Learn to cook chicken yakisoba for my friends by the end of the month" gives you enough time to practice and learn.

However, you still need to break this down into further stages to increase your likelihood of success.

For example, this goal can be broken down into manageable stages:

- ✓ Find recipes by the end of this week.
- ✓ Practice at least three recipes one time each.
- ✓ When I find one I like, I'll practice it again before I invite my friends over.

8. Determine the Where

It can be helpful to identify a particular place where you will work on achieving your goal. For example, if your goal is to exercise three times a week, you would want to determine whether you will go to a gym, exercise at home, or go running in a park.

In our example, you could decide to start by attending a cooking class or choose to do the whole process in your kitchen.

9. Determine the How

This step encourages you to envision how you will achieve each stage of the goal process. This clearly defines the goal's framework and gives you a good sense of what actions you will need to take at each stage.

For the chicken yakisoba example, you would need to find a recipe, obtain the ingredients, get the necessary tools, and make time to practice the dish.

10. Determine the Why

As mentioned earlier, you are more likely to achieve your goal if you find it meaningful and are motivated to work toward it. This question will help you clarify what your motivation is to reach this goal. What will achieving this goal do for you?

In our example, you might want to learn to cook chicken yakisoba for your friends so that you can invite them over to share a special meal with them. Doing this will allow you to bond with your friends and show them how much you care about them.

It is essential to keep this *"why"* in mind as you work toward achieving your goals. Setting concrete, specific goals is helpful, but you also need to keep the big picture in mind.

11. Word your goals positively

Research shows that you are more likely to achieve your goals when they are framed as positive. In other words, articulate your goals as something you are working toward, not something you want to move away from.

For example, if one of your goals is to eat more healthy foods, an unhelpful way to word this might be "Stop eating junk food." This way of wording makes it seem like you are being deprived of something, and humans don't like that feeling.

Instead, try wording the goal as something you are gaining or learning: "Eat at least three servings of fruits and vegetables every day."

12. Make sure that your goals are performance-based

Achieving your goals requires hard work and motivation, but you also need to ensure that you're setting goals that are possible from the hard work you are doing. You can only control your actions, not their outcomes (or others' actions).

Keeping your goals focused on what actions you can take, rather than on specific outcomes, will also help when you experience setbacks. By defining success as a series of steps, you will feel that you are accomplishing your goals even when you don't necessarily get the desired outcome.

For example, "Become Prime Minister" is a goal that relies on the outcome of the actions of others (in this case, voters). You cannot control these actions, and thus, this goal is problematic. However, "Run for elected office" is achievable because it relies on your own motivation and work. Even if you do not win the election, you can view your accomplishment as a success.

Personal and Professional Development

I would recommend that you dedicate a minimum of 30 minutes every day to personal/professional development. Your business's progression depends on how you and others within your organisation progress and how you grow. This is not physically (larger office, more real estate etc.) but mentally. You see, "You don't know what you don't know". In all my years' experience, the number one reason for a business NOT delivering all it is capable of providing is that the business owner doesn't know how to or have the confidence to let it!

Let me explain. As an international motivational business speaker, I have addressed business owner audiences worldwide, predominantly about business SCALE. I already know that in every audience, at every event, there will be three types of business owner. Whilst I am trying to appeal to all three, there will be one group that is far more successful because of my input than the other two groups!

Group 1 – Conference Junkies

They are the nicest possible people. They arrive early, and stay until the very end, always engage and ask questions, and are model attendees. But, contrary to popular belief, their business is slowly making little progress. You see, they are in LEARN mode and are so caught up in the 'must learn new stuff' that they fail to allow much of this to sink in and understand how to implement what they have learnt into their business.

They have lots of knowledge but little to no experience in implementation and, as a result, their business suffers.

Group 2 – Implementation Junkies

Time is not on their side. They arrive late and leave early. They fidget throughout the presentation and often get frustrated with others asking questions. These are the group just itching to implement. As soon as you have uttered the words, they are on their laptops, tablets, or phones, making changes right there and then.

You would be mistaken to think these are flying in their business. They are not! These are the ones that jump from idea to idea, so rapidly implementing everything they learn, they forget to determine and filter IF and HOW it is relevant, instead of believing, *"If it worked for him, it will work for me too"*. They often become frustrated and confused as to why the millions the speaker has generated isn't suddenly falling into their bank accounts also!

Group 3 – Think THEN Act.

Sadly, this group are often the smallest contingent in the room. They arrive on time, they do not stay beyond the expected finish time, and they may or may not buy something from you at the event.

These people are thinkers. They stop, consider, review, and then implement. And as a result, often sail silently past both the junky groups.

Continual learning, putting time aside daily for you to work on YOU, has never been more critical, and the more frequently you allocate some time, the quicker you will begin to see impactful results!

Continuing Professional Development

Continuing Professional Development (CPD) develops professional skills and knowledge through interactive, participation-based, or independent learning. It enables learners to proactively build their professional capabilities through certified education or self-guided learning methods.

CPD involves setting objectives for short- and long-term progression with a structured and goal-specific plan. Records of any CPD should be kept so that you can reflect on the knowledge attained, track progress and provide evidence of the learning.

Development should build on technical and non-technical skills to gain the expertise and understanding required to approach professional situations from various angles.

CPD can also be an excellent self-motivation tool, as it reminds you of your achievements and progression. Plus, its flexibility and diversity – in terms of the different forms of CPD learning available – allows you to find a learning approach that fits you best.

CPD benefits for the business:
- ✓ You don't know what you don't know (as they say in the Army, any time spent in 'recce' is seldom wasted!)
- ✓ Learning from other business leaders/business sectors can help understand how others overcome challenges and highlight challenges you may not yet have faced, therefore preparing you or teaching you how to avoid them.
- ✓ Ensures that standards throughout the company are consistently high.
- ✓ Improves efficiency and productivity with highly skilled and motivated staff.

- ✓ Enhances the business's reputation among customers and clients as well as potential employees.
- ✓ Promotes a healthy learning culture.
- ✓ Improves retention as the team feel valued and loyal.
- ✓ Provides a valuable benchmark for annual reviews and appraisals.
- ✓ Enables the company to react positively and move with current trends and shifts in the industry.

To achieve these benefits, businesses should always support employees' continuous personal development and allow equal access to learning opportunities.

What are the Different Types of CPD?
There are two main types of CPD: formal, structured learning and informal, self-directed learning.

- ✓ Formal CPD usually follows set curriculums, often approved by professional bodies such as the CPD Certification Service, to prove they are effective and well-structured.
- ✓ Conversely, informal CPD involves learners engaging in independent professional learning by finding their own sources of information and activities.

Formal CPD: structured, active learning
For the business owner, this may well be the support of a business coach/mentor. Engaging in either group or 1:1 learning (Such as Masterclasses or a Mastermind).

Informal CPD: unstructured, self-directed learning
Self-directed learning refers to any development activities guided solely by the learner, often without following a curriculum. If you are going to engage in self-directed CPD, you should draw up a CPD plan covering what you expect to learn.

Self-directed CPD includes:

- ✓ Studying online and offline publications written by industry experts.
- ✓ Reading articles and case studies.
- ✓ Listening to and making notes on podcasts.
- ✓ Following industry-specific newsfeeds.
- ✓ Writing articles and essays for personal development; and
- ✓ Additional studying and revising for professional examinations.

Learners should aim to engage in both formal and informal CPD to achieve the benefits of both.

It is also crucial that learners reflect on their CPD learning. It is the most critical stage of the CPD process, as it enables you to determine what worked and where your strengths lie, and how you can plan and improve future CPD activities. Self-reflection is practised by those who are genuinely goal-oriented and open to real growth.

Point to note: *Whilst formal CPD does still lurk in the corridors of giant PLC's. A lot less credence is given to this these days since the explosion of digitally delivered learning. Therefore, whilst many large organisations still insist on this within their KPI requirements. More forward-thinking businesses worldwide have already shifted to making far more use of and recognising more informal style learning.*

Mindset & Motivation: Conclusion

Before embarking on implementing any change within the business, it is vital to determine what you want to achieve from this? How do you measure success? How will you know you are on track to achieving it?

It is crucial you have clarity on what you want to achieve in life, that your business can then be tailored to enable that to become a reality.

Be that more money, more time, more freedom, all three or something completely different.

As the owner/leader within the business, you get to choose. The trick here is to choose wisely and with consideration for what that means.

Only once you have done this work can we begin work to determine if the business is assigned to deliver this for you and, if not, what is required to change, amend, or start/stop for this to be the outcome.

However, it is also essential to determine precisely what that looks like for the business and not just you. There is an enormous responsibility attached to growing a significant and sustainable business. Far beyond any 'get rich quick' promise! To scale sustainably, we must ensure that what we put in place is not solely reliant on us but a proactive and working team towards a common goal. And that this goal is beyond your aspirations of success. That it can continue to grow and thrive beyond your involvement within it.

So, few business owners start with the end in mind, and yet without giving this sufficient consideration, there is little to no chance of ever achieving all of which you and the business are capable!

Further reading

If you would like to learn more about WHY there are two fabulous books by Dr Simon Sinek:

Start with WHY - How Great Leaders Inspire Everyone to Take Action (Dr Simon Sinek)

Finding your Why - A Practical Guide to Discovering Purpose for You and Your Team (Simon Sinek)

Another great read regarding setting your business up is :
The E-Myth Revisited - Why Most Small Businesses Don't Work and What to Do About It (Michael E. Gerber)

Within my top 5 Business Books, is by Napoleon Hill entitled **'Think and grow rich**.' It is well worth a read (if you haven't already) understanding more about personal and business goals and the importance of mindset, sharing your goals with others, and collective
accountability.

And, you might also like to read my second book:
Road2Utopia (and how to take a shortcut)

Chapter two:

Vision, Culture, Values and Purpose

There is a significant and considered difference between businesses that do OK and companies that do far more. And it starts WAY BEFORE the doors open for the first time and the business begins to trade.

If you want you and your business to do well, achieve great things, and provide significantly for you, your family, your employees and your community, it has to be more than a business – it has to have a WHY.

Setting out a VISION for what you want the business to achieve, determining the culture you want to accomplish within the company, setting values to which the business will operate, and clearly defining the businesses' purpose are all milestones in achieving this.

Business Vision

A carefully crafted **Vision Statement** is at the heart of every successful business. This statement clearly and concisely communicates your business's overall goals and can serve as a tool for strategic decision making across the company.

A **Vision Statement** can be as simple as a single sentence or can span a short paragraph. Regardless of the individual details and nuances, all effective vision statements define the core ideals that give a business shape and direction. These statements also provide a powerful way to motivate and guide employees.

Why does this matter?
Research shows that employees who find their company's vision meaningful have engagement levels of 68 per cent, which is 19 points above average. More engaged employees are often more productive and can be more effective corporate ambassadors in the larger community.

Given the impact that a vision statement can have on a company's long-term success and even its bottom line, it is worth taking the time to craft a statement that synthesizes your ambition and mobilizes your staff.

Vision statement vs mission statement
Before determining what your vision statement will be, you need to understand what it is not. It should not be confused with a Mission Statement.

Mission Statement

A Mission Statement is based in the present and is designed to convey to both the company and the external community a sense of why the company exists.

Vision Statements are future-based and are meant to inspire and give direction to the company's employees rather than to customers.

A Mission Statement answers the question "*Why does my business exist?*" while a Vision Statement answers the question "*Where do I see my business going*?"

So, let's be quite clear:

A vision is an aspiration. A mission is actionable.

Who will shape your vision, and how will it be used?
The first step in writing a vision statement is determining who will play a role in crafting it. The best way to develop a vision statement is through a series of workshops with key stakeholders representing your organisation's cross-section. Teams of people can craft alternate versions of the statement and receive feedback from the rest of the group.

What is a Stakeholder?

A stakeholder is anyone with an interest in a business. Stakeholders are individuals, groups or organisations that are affected by the activity of the company.

They include:

- ✓ Owners who are interested in how much profit the business makes.
- ✓ Managers who are concerned about their salary.
- ✓ Workers who want to earn high wages and keep their jobs.
- ✓ Customers who want the business to produce quality products at reasonable prices.
- ✓ Suppliers who want the business to continue to buy their products.
- ✓ Lenders who want to be repaid on time and in full.
- ✓ The community has a stake in the business as employers of local people. Business activity also affects the local

environment. For example, noisy night-time deliveries or a smelly factory would be unpopular with residents.

Internal stakeholders are groups within a business, e.g. owners and workers. External stakeholders are groups outside a company - e.g. the community.

Individual stakeholder interviews can also offer another effective way to get real and honest feedback in which people will not hold back on how they feel. This can only truly be enabled by creating a business culture where people feel safe in doing so.

Additionally, a business should determine early how its vision statement will appear and its role in the organisation. This will prevent the process from becoming merely an intellectual exercise.

The vision business statement should be thought of as part of your strategic plan. It is an internal communications tool that helps align and inspire your team to reach its goals.

As such, vision statements should be viewed as living documents that will be revisited and revised.

How to write a vision statement

Writing your vision statement is a time for creativity, ambition, and fun, but the task should be approached seriously.

There is a process to this, and it's not usually quick or straightforward. The best way to begin is to reflect on some of the most significant events or ideas that have impacted the company.

How to write a Vision Statement:

To begin, first, identify the core values of the organisation when crafting your vision statement. Then, ask yourself:

What do we do right now that aligns with these values? Where are we not aligned with these values? How can we stay aligned with these values as we grow over the next five years, ten years?

Those questions address your current situation and help identify the bigger-picture vision.

Next, ask yourself:

What problems your company hopes to solve in the next few years? What does your company hope to achieve? Who is your target customer base, and what do you want to do for them?

Based on your responses to these questions, ask yourself:

What will success look like if you accomplish those things? This answer should shape your vision statement.

A vision statement should also be concise, no longer than a sentence or a few paragraphs. You want your entire team and organisation to be able to repeat it back easily and, more importantly, understand it. But a vision statement should be more than a catchy tagline.

It can be smart and memorable, but this is for your team and culture, not for selling a specific product.

When you are crafting your vision statement, dream big. Do not worry about practicality for now.
What initially looks impossible could be achieved down the road

with the right team and technologies. Work on shaping a vision statement that reflects the specific nature of your business.

There is nothing wrong with a vision statement being a little daring, distinct or even disagreeable.

If a vision statement sets out a generic goal that anyone can agree with, it is likely to produce mediocre results. A goal like 'delivering an exceptional experience' applies equally to a hospital, a bank, or a fitness club.

> ### Tips for crafting your vision statement:
>
> ✓ *Project five to ten years in the future.*
> ✓ *Dream big and focus on success.*
> ✓ *Use the present tense.*
> ✓ *Use clear, concise language.*
> ✓ *Infuse your vision statement with passion and emotion.*
> ✓ *Paint a mental picture of the business you want.*
> ✓ *Have a plan to communicate your vision statement to your employees.*
> ✓ *Be prepared to commit time and resources to the vision you establish.*
>
> *Involve your stakeholders at every stage of the process.*

Vision statements should stretch the imagination while providing direction and clarity. A good vision statement will help inform the direction and set priorities while challenging employees to grow. The vision statement should be compelling not just to the high-level execs of your company but also to all employees.

Your completed vision statement will give your employees a clear idea of your company's path forward. Then, it's up to you to nurture and support that vision and to inspire your employees to do the same.

What is a Mission Statement?

With all this talk of a **Vision Statement**, we could become either complacent or confused about the need or purpose of a Mission Statement!

A **Mission Statement** is a sentence describing a company's function, markets, and competitive advantages; a short written statement of your business goals and philosophies

A **Mission Statement** defines what an organisation is, why it exists, and its reason for being. At a minimum, your mission statement should explain who your primary customers are, identify the products and services you produce, and describe the geographical location in which you operate.

If you do not have a mission statement, create one by writing your business's purpose in one sentence. Ask two or three of the key people in your company to do the same thing. Then discuss the statements and come up with one sentence everyone agrees with. Once you have finalised your mission statement, communicate it to everyone in the company.

It is more important to communicate the mission statement to employees than to customers. Your mission statement does not have to be creative or catchy – just accurate.

If you already have a mission statement, you will need to review it annually and possibly revise it to reflect your company's goals accurately. The business and economic climates evolve. To do this, ask yourself if the statement still correctly describes what you are doing.

If your review results in a revision of the statement, be sure everyone in the company knows the change. Make a big deal out of it. After all, a change in your mission probably means your company is growing – and that is a big deal.

Once you have designed a niche for your business, you are ready to create a mission statement. A key tool that can be as important as your business plan, a mission statement captures the essence of your business's goals and the philosophies underlying them in a few succinct sentences. Equally important, the mission statement signals what your business is all about to your customers, employees, suppliers, and the community.

The mission statement reflects every facet of your business: the range and nature of the products you offer, pricing, quality, service, marketplace position, growth potential, use of technology, and your relationships with your customers, employees, suppliers, competitors and the community.

Do not waste your time with a bad mission statement

Because a traditional business plan includes a mission statement, that is not a reason to do one. If it is not going to be useful for you and help guide your business, don't bother. Most mission statements are just meaningless hype that could be used to describe any business.

Do not fall into the trap of writing a mission statement just because some checklist or expert said you had to. You should write a mission statement if you want to add clarity to your business goals. You want to get your employees, investors, and customers to understand what your organisation is all about.

If you already have a mission statement and you want to see if it is adding value to your organisation, try to have it pass this simple test:

Ask yourself, honestly, whether your competitors could use the same statement.

Does it distinguish you from all other businesses? If you gave an employee or customer a blind screening test, asking them to read your mission statement and four others without identifying which would they be able to tell which mission statement was yours?

Define your mission statement to develop your business. Write a business plan that reflects your mission.

How to write a great mission statement

So how do you create a good mission statement? Over the decades I have spent reading, writing, and evaluating business plans, I have come up with a process for developing a good mission statement, and it boils down to five steps.

1. Start with a market-defining story.

You do not have to write the story — it is not included in the mission statement — but think it through because it will guide how you write your mission statement:

Imagine a real person deciding to buy what you sell. Use your imagination to see why they want it, how they find you, and what buying from you does for them. The more concrete the story, the better. And keep that in mind for the actual mission statement wording: "The more concrete, the better."

A good market-defining story explains the need, or the want, or—if you like jargon—the so-called "why to buy." It defines the target customer or "buyer persona." And it illustrates how your business is different from most others or even unique. It simplifies thinking about what a company isn't, what it doesn't do.

This is not part of the mission statement. Instead, it is a vital thing to have in your head while you write the mission statement. It's in the background, between the words.

If you are having trouble getting started, make a quick list of what your company does and doesn't do.

2. Define what your business does for its customers.

Start your mission statement with the good you do. Use your market-defining story to check out whatever it is that makes your business special for your target customer.

Do not undervalue your business: You do not have to cure cancer or stop global climate change to be doing good.

This is a part of your mission statement and a crucial element at that—write it down.

If your business is good for the world, incorporate that here too. But, there are claims about being good for the world to be meaningful and distinguishable from all the other businesses.

Add the words "clean" or "green" only if that is true, and you keep to it rigorously. Do not just say it, especially if it is not important or always valid.

For example, Apple Computer's 2020 mission statement is:

> *Apple revolutionized personal technology with the introduction of the Macintosh in 1984. Today, Apple leads the world in innovation with iPhone, iPad, Mac, Apple Watch, and Apple TV. Apple's four software platforms— iOS, macOS, watchOS, and tvOS—provide seamless experiences across all Apple devices and empower people with breakthrough services, including the App Store, Apple Music, Apple Pay, and iCloud. Apple's more than 100,000 employees are dedicated to making the best products on earth and to leaving the world better than we found it.*

That one passes the test of defining the company with flying colours. Nobody could mistake that mission with generic hype.

And it is an exciting change from the early mission as defined by founder Steve Jobs:

> *To contribute to the world by making tools for the mind that advance humankind.*

On the other hand, Ikea starts its mission statement with something that could be any company anywhere. "Our vision is to create a better everyday life for many people." To its credit, it goes on to define a "rest of the mission" that could only be IKEA:

> *We make this possible by offering a wide range of well-designed, functional home furnishing products at prices so low that as many people as possible will be able to afford them.*

3. Define what your business does for its employees.

Profitable businesses are good for their employees too, or they simply do not last. Keeping employees is better for the bottom line than turnover. Company culture matters. Rewarding and motivating people matters.

A mission statement can define what your business offers its employees.

My recommendation is that you do not merely assert how the business is right for employees—you define it here and then forever after, making it accurate.

Qualities like fairness, diversity, respect for ideas and creativity, training, tools, empowerment, and the like really matter. However, since every business in existence says that it prioritises those things, strive for a differentiator and make the general goals feel more concrete and specific.

With this part of the mission statement, there is a built-in dilemma. On the one hand, everybody is desirable to use the mission statement to establish what you want for employees in your business. On the other hand, it is hard to do that without falling into the trap of saying what every other company says.

Stating that you value fair compensation, room to grow, training, a healthy, creative work environment, and respect for diversity is probably a good idea, even if that part of your mission statement is not unique.

That is because the mission statement can serve as a reminder—for owners, supervisors, and workers—and as a lever for self-enforcement.

If you have a particular view on your relationship with employees, write it into the mission statement. If your business is friendly to families, or remote virtual workplaces, put that into your mission – as this is rare in mission statements. The majority are focused on messaging for customers. My recommendation here is not the norm. I include it because it is good practice, even though not common.

Apple differentiated its goals of training and empowering employees by making a point of bringing in very high-quality educators and presenters to help employees' business expertise grow. That was part of the culture and, to my mind, part of the mission, but it was not part of the mission statement, although it easily could (and perhaps should) have been.

American Express, however, includes the team in its mission:

We have a mission to be the world's most respected service brand. To do this, we have established a culture that supports our team members so that they can provide exceptional service to our customers.

4. Add what the business does for its owners.

In business school, it is taught that management's mission is to enhance the stock's value. And shares of stock are ownership. Some would say that a business exists to enrich its owners' financial position, and maybe it does. However, only a small subset of all companies is about the business buzzwords of *"share value"* and *"return on investment."*

In the early years of my first business, I wanted growth more than peace of mind about cash flow. So, I wrote that into my mission statement. And at one point, I realised I was also building a business that was a place where I was happy to be working with people I wanted to work with, so I wrote that into my mission statement too.

However, this element, as with the suggestion about including employees, is unusual. Few mission statements do it. That is understandable since most mission statements are outward-facing only, aimed at customers and nobody else.

5.   Discuss, digest, cut, polish, review, revise.

Whatever you wrote for points two, three and four above, go back and cut down the wordiness.

Good mission statements serve multiple functions, define objectives, and live for a long time. So, edit. This step is so worthwhile.

Start by considering developing a complete mission statement for internal use and using a customer-facing subset for general publication. That is common. Many companies have segmented mission statements, with sections set aside and categorised by type or goal. Use bullet points or sections if that works for you. People confuse mission with vision because many businesses use them together, and many others also redefine them to fit their context. So, what a company does for customers is often called vision, despite the formal definition.

Remember, form follows function in mission statements, as in all business writing. Make it work for your business. Or don't do it at all. If you want to call it a vision that works for employees and customers, then do that.

As you edit, keep a sharp eye out for the buzzwords and hype that everybody claims. Cut as much as you can that does not apply specifically to your business, except for the occasional particular elements that—unique or not—can serve as long-term rules and reminders. The word 'unique' itself means, literally, the only one in the world. Use it sparingly. Phrases such as "being the best possible," "world-class," and "great customer service" mean little because everybody uses them. Having excellent customer service (as we discuss further in the book) is way harder than writing that into a mission statement.

It may help if you choose to read other companies' mission statements before writing a statement about you and not some other company. Make sure you believe in your writing— Your customers and your employees will soon spot a lie, exaggeration, or desire.

Then listen. Show drafts to others, ask their opinions and actively listen. Do not argue, do not convince them, just listen. And then edit again.

And, for the rest of your business's life, review and revise it as needed. As with everything in a business plan, your mission statement should never get written in stone and, much less, stashed in a drawer. Use it or lose it. Review and revise as necessary because change is constant.

Culture Statement

Everyone loves company culture. And everyone loves metrics. However, business leaders have had a hard time putting the two together in a meaningful way. Culture has long been regarded as a "soft" topic – too intangible, subjective, and elusive to measure and track.

This has made it challenging to know how to align culture with business success.

However, if the fundamental principles of the company's culture are compiled in a single **Culture Statement** that everyone can read and understand. Then this provides an ideal base from which to build.

The Culture Statement is comparable to a playbook that provides your team with a clear overview of what culture looks like in your business. It may be in the form of a handbook, a digital deck, or a narrative statement. The Culture Statement is a compilation of your business's mission, values, traditions, and beliefs. It will be used to guide your team in their actions, priorities, and decisions.

All employees must understand the company culture. The company culture statement should be introduced to new employees as early as possible, preferably during the onboarding process. Ongoing training initiatives will ensure that employees remain aligned with the path and purpose of the organisation. Some businesses introduce their culture statement to prospective employees during the interview as part of the screening process. It is a helpful tool to explain the "why" behind the business's operations and help determine fit.

The benefits of a strong corporate culture are both intuitive and supported by social science. (Heskett, 8 Aug 2011)

> *Culture can account for 20-30% of the differential in corporate performance compared with 'culturally unremarkable' competitors.*

Typical components of a Valued Company Culture

But what makes a culture? Each culture is unique, and many factors go into creating one, but I have observed at least six standard components of great cultures. Isolating those elements can be the first step to building a differentiated culture and a lasting organisation.

Vision

A great culture starts with a **vision statement,** as discussed previously; these simple turns of phrase guide a company's values and provides it with purpose. That purpose, in turn, orients every decision employees make. When they are deeply authentic and prominently displayed, good vision statements can even help customers, suppliers, and other stakeholders to understand HOW we do what we do. Non-profits often excel at having compelling, simple vision statements. The Alzheimer's Association, for example, is dedicated to *"a world without Alzheimer's."* And Oxfam envisions *"a just world without poverty."* A vision statement is a simple but foundational element of culture.

Values

A company's values are the core of its culture. While a vision articulates a company's purpose, values offer a set of guidelines on the behaviours and mindsets needed to achieve that vision. For example, McKinsey & Company has a clearly articulated set of values that are prominently communicated to all employees and includes firm vows to serve clients, treat colleagues, and uphold professional standards. Google's values might be best articulated by their famous phrase, *"Don't be evil."* But they are also enshrined in their *"Ten things we know to be true."* And while many companies find their values revolve around a few simple topics (employees, clients, professionalism, etc.), those values' originality is less important than their authenticity.

Practices

Of course, values are of little importance unless they are enshrined in a company's practices. If an organisation professes "people are our greatest asset", it should also be ready to invest in people in visible ways. Similarly, if an organisation values a *"flat"* hierarchy, it must encourage more junior team members to contribute to discussions without fear or negative repercussions. And whatever an organisation's values, they must be reinforced in review criteria and promotion policies and baked into the firm's operating principles of daily life.

People

No company can build a coherent culture without people who either share its core values or possess the willingness and ability to embrace those values. That is why the greatest firms in the world also have some of the most stringent recruiting policies. According to Charles Ellis, the best firms are: *"Fanatical about recruiting new employees who are not just the most talented but also the best suited to a particular corporate culture."* ('What it Takes: Seven Secrets of Success from the World's Greatest Professional Firms' (D.Ellis, 25 Jan 2013)

Ellis highlights that those firms often have 8-20 people interview each candidate. And as an added benefit, Steven Hunt notes at Monster.com that one study found applicants who were a cultural fit would accept a 7% lower salary. Departments with cultural alignment had 30% less turnover. (Coleman, 2013) People stick with cultures they like and bring on the right "culture carriers" to reinforce the organisation's culture. (Hunt, n.d.)

Narrative

Marshall Ganz was once a key part of Caesar Chavez's United Farm Workers movement and helped structure the organising platform for Barack Obama's 2008 presidential campaign. Now a professor at Harvard, one of Ganz's core areas of research and teaching is narrative power. Any organization has a unique history, a unique story. And the ability to unearth that history and craft it into a narrative is a core element of culture creation. The elements of that narrative can be formal, like Coca-Cola, which dedicated an enormous resource to celebrating its heritage and even has a World of Coke museum in Atlanta. Or informal, like those stories about how Steve Jobs' early fascination in calligraphy shaped the aesthetically oriented culture at Apple. But they are more powerful when identified, shaped, and retold as a part of a firm's ongoing culture.

Place

Why does Pixar have a vast open atrium engineering environment where firm members run into each other throughout the day and interact in informal, unplanned ways? Why does Mayor Michael Bloomberg prefer his staff sit in a *"bullpen"* environment rather than one of the separate offices with soundproof doors? And why do tech firms cluster in Silicon Valley and financial firms cluster in London and New York? There are numerous answers to each of these questions, but one clear answer is that place shapes culture. Open architecture is more conducive to certain office behaviours, like collaboration. Certain cities and countries have local cultures that may reinforce or contradict the culture a firm is trying to create. Place - whether geography, architecture, or aesthetic design - impacts people's values and behaviours in the workplace.

These six components can provide a firm foundation for shaping a new organisation's culture. And identifying and understanding them more fully in an existing organisation can be the first step to revitalizing or reshaping culture in a company looking for a change.

The components should be reflected in a clear and accepted culture statement which is disseminated throughout the business.

Considerations when writing a Culture Statement.

Communication

In companies with strong communication, employees can communicate their thoughts and suggestions to the leadership, while the leadership effectively communicates necessary information to employees. Assess if your current communication channels effectively help everyone in the company send, receive, and understand data.

Innovation

As an entrepreneur, innovation is one of my favourite subjects. It is closely related to communication because it comes down to whether employees can move ideas through the organisation and how much your company is open to new ideas. When measuring innovation, remember that it comes in many forms, such as resources, processes, behaviours, and the product itself.

Agility

Agility is key to staying competitive in the market. Whilst the leadership might feel that they are adapting well to internal and external changes, other employees will be the ones to feel the effects of whatever falls through the cracks.
Therefore, track your company's agility by regularly soliciting feedback from employees at all levels.

Wellness

Workplace wellness encompasses the mental and physical health of employees. Wellness leads to happier and more productive employees, but this metric also has a significant ripple effect. According to a 2018 study, medical costs and absentee costs fall about £3.27 and £2.73 respectively for every pound spent on wellness programs. (Gustavsson, 2018)

Environment

While it is undoubtedly exciting, you do not need to have a trendy or themed office to have an effective work environment.

What is most important is that the workplace provides for comfortable, productive employees. For instance, small details, such as the office's temperature, could be resulting in significant losses in productivity. Focus on employee comments related to the workplace, and you will find some of the easiest and fastest ways to improve their performance.

Collaboration

Collaboration has many layers, and once again, employee feedback is the key to getting to the bottom of them. Your marketing team might work splendidly together but struggle to work with other departments. To fully measure your company's collaboration, look for collaboration within teams and collaboration between teams.

Support

Employees should feel supported by the overall company, their manager, and peers. According to a Harvard Business Review study (Rogers, 2018), middle managers are the most disgruntled group in the workforce, possibly because they lack the support they need to be successful.

By digging into this metric on an individual and group level, you will be able to expose essential trends in engagement.

Performance focus

Everyone should understand what determines success in their role, and they should be rewarded or recognised accordingly. More significant rewards do not necessarily make for a more robust culture. Instead, take time to understand if employees feel appreciated and how they would like to be recognised.

Responsibility

Responsibility encompasses employee accountability for actions and results and the ability to make decisions regarding their work. While it seems like an individual metric, these behaviours should be promoted and assessed on a company-wide level. And believe me, you will find that employees are eager to report back on their experience in this area.

Mission and value alignment

The first step is having a mission statement and company values, and that is the easy part. You should also keep regular tabs on whether employees know your mission and values, understand them, and live by them. This process starts during recruitment, so do not let this metric fall to the wayside during high growth periods.

So, there you have it; finally, culture and metrics can live happily ever after. The unique way you approach these qualities is what I like to call your company's *"personality"*. These metrics will not capture your personality's specifics, but they will measure if it is working for your employees. They will help you understand if your culture contributes to a happy, engaged, and effective workforce.

Values Statement

Business values are the core principles or standards that guide the way you do business. They sum up what your company stands for and what makes it special. While business plans and strategies may change, the core values of your business remain the same.

For example, some businesses say that innovation is one of their core values - they are continually developing new products or services, shaping their whole business approach. Other companies may say that they are agile - they are always responding to change and creating new customers opportunities.

Every business is different and will have its own set of values - whether these are articulated may well influence the business's success level in retaining both staff and customers.

Want proof?

Here is what happened at a recent management conference held by a financial services company. The CEO began by proudly announcing the important role that a new set of corporate values—teamwork, quality, and innovation—would play at the firm. He then showed a slick video that illustrated each word with stock footage of world-class athletes, swelling music, and shots of employees waving awkwardly at the camera. The whole effort reeked of insincerity. When the CEO cheerfully asked audience members if they wanted to watch it again, he was met by a loud chorus of *"No!"* It was painfully clear that his credibility was shot.

Given the risk, why do executives put so much work into developing values statements in the first place? Because they believe they must. At least, that is how they had felt since 1994 when Jim Collins and Jerry Porras published *Built to Last*. (Collin / Porras, 1994) The book made the case that many of the best companies adhered to a set of principles called core values, provoking managers to stampede to off-site meetings to conjure up some core values of their own.

The values fad swept through corporate America like chicken pox through a kindergarten class. Today, 80% of the Fortune 100 tout their values publicly—values that too often stand for nothing but a desire to be chic or, worse still, politically correct.

The debasement of values is a shame, not only because the resulting cynicism poisons the cultural well but also because it wastes a great opportunity. Values can set a company apart from the competition by clarifying its identity and serving as a rallying point for employees.

But coming up with solid values (and sticking to them) requires real guts. Indeed, an organisation considering a values initiative must first come to terms with the fact that values inflict pain when properly practised. They make some employees feel like outcasts – not intentionally. Still, the employees may find themselves reviewing their values and culture and find they do not match that of the organisation. Strong values can limit an organisation's strategic and operational freedom and constrain the behaviour of its people. They leave executives open to heavy criticism for even minor violations. And they demand constant vigilance.

> *"If you're not willing to accept the real pain values incur,*
> *don't bother going to the trouble*
> *of formulating a values statement."*
> **Patrick M. Lencioni, Harvard Business Review**

You will be better off without one. But if you have the fortitude to see the effort through, you can learn some critical lessons from the few companies that have adopted meaningful corporate values. Whether their values stemmed directly from their founders' vision and character or were developed later through formal programs, these companies all followed four fundamental imperatives in creating and implementing their values.

1. *Core values are the deeply ingrained principles that guide all a company's actions; they serve as its cultural cornerstones. Collins and Porras succinctly define core values as inherent and sacrosanct; they can never be compromised, either for convenience or short-term economic gain.*

2. *Aspirational values are those that a company needs to succeed in the future but currently lacks. A company may need to develop a new value to support a new strategy or meet a changing market or industry requirements.*
   2.1. *Aspirational values need to be carefully managed to ensure that they do not dilute the core. For example, there was a company with a core value that recognised extreme hard work and dedication. Its employees were known to work late into the evenings and on weekends.*

> At some point, the executive team felt compelled to add "work-life balance" as an aspirational value. Still, they ultimately decided against it because doing so would confuse employees about what mattered most to the company.

3. Permission-to-play values reflect the minimum behavioural and social standards required of any employee. They tend not to vary much across companies, particularly those working in the same region or industry, which means that, by definition, they never really help distinguish a company from its competitors.

   3.1. It can often become confusing when leaders confuse core values with permission-to-play values. For example: Insisting that integrity was a core value of the company. Unless a company is willing to adopt unusually tough measures to demonstrate that it held a higher standard of integrity than most companies, integrity should be classified as a permission-to-play value, not a core one.

4. Accidental values arise spontaneously without being cultivated by leadership and take hold over time.
   They usually reflect the common interests or personalities of the organisation's employees. Accidental values can be good for a company, such as when they create an atmosphere of inclusivity. But they can also be opposing forces, foreclosing new opportunities by dismissing opportunity if it appears not to meet either aspirational or permission-to-play values fully.

Many companies view a values initiative in the same way they view a marketing launch: a one-time event measured by the initial attention it receives, not the authenticity of its content.

For a values statement to be authentic, it does not have to sound like it belongs on a Hallmark card. Indeed, some of the most values-driven companies adhere to tough, if not downright, controversial values.

Own the Process.

What is the first thing many executives do after they decide to embark on a values initiative?

They hand off the HR department's effort, which uses the initiative as an excuse for an inclusive feel-good effort. To engage employees, HR rolls out employee surveys and holds lots of town meetings to gather input and build consensus.

That is precisely the wrong approach. Values initiatives have nothing to do with building consensus—they are about imposing a set of fundamental, strategically sound beliefs on a broad group of people.

Most executives understand the danger of consensus-driven decision making when it comes to strategy, finance, and other business issues. Yet, they seem oblivious to the problem when it comes to developing values. Surveying all employees about what values they believe the company should adopt is a bad idea for two reasons. First, it integrates suggestions from many employees who probably do not belong at the company in the first place.
And second, it creates the false impression that all input is equally valuable.

The best-valued efforts are driven by small teams that include the CEO, any founders who are still with the company, and a handful of key employees.

Weave Core Values into Everything

Let's say you have nailed down the right values. What now? Suppose they are going to really take hold in your organisation. In that case, your core values need to be integrated into every employee-related process—hiring methods, performance management systems, criteria for promotions and rewards, and even dismissal policies.

From the first interview to the last day of work, employees should be continuously reminded that core values form the basis of every company's decision.

Given all the hard work that goes into developing and implementing a solid values system, most companies would probably prefer not to bother. And indeed, they should not, because poorly executed values can poison a company's culture.

Make no mistake, living by stated corporate values is difficult. After all, it is much harder to be clear and unapologetic for what you stand for than to cave into politically correct pressures. And for organisations trying to repair the damage caused by bad values programs, the work is even harder. But if you are willing to devote your time and energy to creating an authentic values statement, there is a good chance that the resulting values will stand your company in far better stead than your competition!

When writing a value proposition, I often refer to this formula:

> *We help {your most promising prospects} that {need help with the problems you solve} succeed by {providing the improvement you will deliver}.*

You may wish to go further and include:

> *Unlike {the alternative solution}, {your solution} {describe the reason why your company is a better choice} as demonstrated by {evidence that you will deliver as promised}.*

What is PURPOSE?

We hear more and more that organisations must have a compelling "purpose" — but what does that mean? Aren't there already a host of labels out there that describe organisational direction? Do we need yet another? I think we do. Remember, a vision statement says what the organisation wishes to be like in some years' time.

Senior management is usually drawn up to take the thinking beyond day-to-day activity in a clear, memorable way.

The mission statement describes what business the organisation is in (and what it is not) both now and projecting into the future. It aims to provide the focus for management and staff. A consulting firm might define its mission by the type of work it does, the clients it caters to, and the level of service it provides.

For example: *"We are in the business of providing help, support, guidance and accountability to business leaders and business owners dedicated to the significant and sustainable SCALE of both them and their businesses."*

Values describe the desired culture. As Coca-Cola puts it, they serve as a behavioural compass. Coke's values include having the courage to shape a better future, leveraging collective genius, being real, and being accountable and committed.

If values provide the compass, purpose gives employees a set of directions. The global logistics and mail service company TNT Express illustrates the difference in its use of both terms. TNT United Kingdom, the European market leader, lists *"customer care"* among nine fundamental principles, describing it as follows: *"Always listening to and building first-class relationships with our customers to help us provide excellent standards of service and client satisfaction."*

TNT's Australian branch takes a different approach. Rather than outline detailed principles, it highlights four high-level *"core values,"* including: *"We are passionate about our customers."* Note the lighter touch.

How does purpose differ from all the above, emphasising how the organisation should view and conduct itself?

If you are crafting a purpose statement, my advice is this:

1. Inspire your staff to do good work for you
2. Find a way to express the organisation's impact on the lives of customers, clients, students, patients — whomever you are trying to serve.
3. Make them feel it long after you have finished delivering your product/service.

Here are a few great examples from global brands:

> **Google**: To organize the world's information and make it universally accessible and useful.
>
> **Kickstarter**: To help bring creative projects to life.
>
> **Tesla**: To accelerate the world's transition to sustainable energy.

Vision, Culture, Values, Purpose: Conclusion

Only you can know what success means for you. For you, your family, and your future. And without first giving this some real consideration as to exactly what it looks, feels, tastes like, it becomes challenging to build a business capable of delivering that to you.

Once this is clear, we can turn our attention to the business. And ensure the business goals, vision, values are aligned to your goal's visions and values sufficiently that you remain motivated and passionate about working to achieve it.

However, these cannot be simply a carbon copy of your personal goals. The business is its own entity and needs its own identity so that it continues to survive and thrive once you have achieved your success. You owe that to the team, customers, clients, and suppliers who enable you to achieve it.

So, set about working with your team to devise a set of vision and values that enable a healthy business culture to form sufficient to deliver these.

Share this with anyone and everyone who has a part to play in making this happen. Learn to live by it; allow it to encapsulate every aspect of who you and what you do. Scale, should you decide to do so, comes from a few years of doing what most others will not, so you can enjoy what most others cannot.

Once you have this completed, it's then time to look at the business and its makeup. To ensure it has the right foundations, right people, systems, processes, the right audience and solutions, and the right level of exchange, along with the right team in place for this to move from the drawing board to your boardroom as a living, breathing reality.

Chapter Three:

Business Strategy and Structure

Business Strategy

The word strategy derives from the Greek word stratēgos, which derives from two words: Stratos (army) and ago (ancient Greek for leading). It could, therefore, be said that a strategy is simply a leadership plan.

The definition of business strategy is a long-term plan of action designed to achieve a goal or set of goals or objectives. A strategy is management's game plan for strengthening the performance of the enterprise. It states how business should be conducted to achieve the desired goals. Without a strategy, management has no roadmap to guide them.

Considerations regarding Business Strategy

There are at least three considerations when it comes to strategy:

- ✓ **Corporate strategy** – The market in which the business shall operate.
- ✓ **Competitive strategy** – How the business shall compete within the market.
- ✓ **Strategy in General** – The glue that ties business plan to business strategy (The What and How)

Strategy in general, refers to how a given objective will be achieved. Consequently, a strategy is concerned with the relationships between ends and means. Between the results we seek and the resources at our disposal. Strategy and tactics are concerned with conceiving and then carrying out courses of action intended to attain objectives. For the most part, your Business strategy is how you deploy or allocate the resources at your disposal, whereas tactics (Business plan) is concerned with how you employ or make use of them. Together, your Business strategy and your Business plan bridge the gap between end results and means of achievement.

Strategy and tactics are terms that originate from the military. Their use in business has required little adaptation as far as a strategy, in general, is concerned. However, corporate strategy and competitive strategy do represent significant departures from the original military definition of strategy.

Strategy and Tactics - Corporate versus Competitive Strategy Corporate strategy defines the markets and the businesses in which a company will operate. Competitive or business strategy establishes the basis on which the business will compete.

Corporate strategy is typically decided through the company's mission and vision. That is, saying what the company does, why it exists, and what it is intended to become. The competitive strategy hinges on a company's capabilities, strengths, and weaknesses in relation to market characteristics and its competitors' corresponding capabilities, strengths, and weaknesses.

According to Michael Porter, a Harvard Business School professor (Porter, 1979) and the reigning guru of competitive strategy, competition within an industry is driven by five primary factors:

- ✓ The threat of new entrants
- ✓ The threat of substitute products or services
- ✓ Bargaining power of suppliers
- ✓ Bargaining power of buyers
- ✓ Rivalry among existing firms

Porter also indicates that, in response to these five factors, a competitive strategy can take one of three generic forms:

- ✓ Focus
- ✓ Differentiation
- ✓ Cost leadership

Factors Affecting Corporate and Competitive Strategy

Several factors can serve as the basis for formulating corporate and competitive strategy. These include:

- ✓ Products/services offered
- ✓ Natural resources
- ✓ Sales-marketing methods
- ✓ Production capacity-capability
- ✓ Users/customers served
- ✓ Size/growth goals
- ✓ Distribution methods
- ✓ Technology
- ✓ Market types and needs
- ✓ Return/profit goals

Michael Treacy and Fred Wiersema (Wiersema, 1997) suggest that "value disciplines" should serve as the basis for settling on strategy (corporate or competitive). The three basic "value disciplines" they present are:

- ✓ **Operational Excellence**: Strategy is predicated on the production and delivery of products and services. The objective is to lead the industry in terms of price and convenience.
- ✓ **Customer Intimacy**: Strategy is predicated on tailoring and shaping products and services to fit an increasing definition of the customer. The objective is long-term customer loyalty and long-term customer profitability.
- ✓ **Product Leadership Generation**: Strategy is predicated on producing a continuous stream of state-of-the-art products and services. The objective is the quick commercialisation of new ideas.

Defining your Business Strategy

A business strategy is concerned with major resource issues, e.g. raising the finance to build a new factory or plant. Strategies are also concerned with deciding what products to allocate significant resources to – for example, when Nissan chose to move its car manufacturing plants from France to the UK.

Strategies are concerned with the scope of a business' activities, i.e., what and where they produce. For example, BIC's scope is focused on three main product areas – lighters, pens, and razors – and they have developed super factories in key geographical locations to produce these items.

Business Strategy Map

A Business strategy map is a great way to see the whole picture on one piece of paper and adjust and align business activities to achieve the company's vision and goals. It takes the systems thinking approach – everything in an organisation and its environment is interrelated and so determines the whole system's outputs. Strategy creation is involved because there are so many interdependencies.

What is a Strategy Map?

A Strategy Map is a drawing that enables you to link actions or objectives into a coherent, logical structure that shows the cause and effect link between your objectives or activities. This is a crucial step in creating a balanced scorecard that brings the management team together into a consensus and gives them a powerful tool to communicate their strategy.

Balanced Scorecard

A balanced scorecard is a strategy performance management tool. A structured report that managers can use to keep track of the execution of activities by the staff within their control. And to monitor the consequences arising from these actions.

The four perspectives of the balanced scorecard:

- ✓ **Financial or Shareholder** –financial results
- ✓ **Customer** – what the customers want or need.
- ✓ **Internal Processes** – the internal organisation and processes that deliver the customer needs.
- ✓ **Learning and Growth** – the training, technology and knowledge needed to operate the processes or procedures successfully.

In each perspective, you define your top objectives and then link them together as the objectives feed into higher objectives.

How to use a Strategy Map

Start with the question 'What?' For example:

What do we want to achieve?

- ✓ **Maintain** Profitability

How are we going to do that?

✓ **Improve** Customer Satisfaction

Now repeat the process

What do we want to achieve?

✓ **Improved** customer satisfaction

How are we going to do that?

✓ **Reduce** support calls, and so on.

Some Fundamental Questions to ask in your Business Strategy

Regardless of the definition of strategy or the many factors affecting the choice of corporate or competitive strategy. There are some fundamental questions to be asked and answered.

These include the following:

✓ Who are we?
✓ What do we do?
✓ Why are we here?
✓ What kind of company are we?
✓ What kind of company do we want to become?
✓ What kind of company must we become?

Related to Strategy in General

✓ What is our objective? What are the ends we seek?
✓ What is our current strategy: implicit or explicit?
✓ What courses of action might lead to the ends we seek?
✓ What are the means at our disposal?
✓ How are our actions restrained and constrained by the means at our disposal?
✓ What risks are involved, and which ones are serious enough that we should plan for them?

Related to Corporate Strategy

✓ What is the current strategy: implicit or explicit?
✓ What assumptions must hold for the current strategy to be viable?
✓ What is happening in the larger social, political, technical, and financial environments?
✓ What are our growth, size, and profitability goals?
✓ In which markets will we compete?
✓ In which businesses will we compete?
✓ In which geographic areas will we compete?

Related to Competitive Strategy

✓ What is the current strategy: implicit or explicit?
✓ What assumptions must hold for the current strategy to be viable?
✓ What is happening in the industry, with our competitors, and in general?
✓ What are our growth, size, and profitability goals?
✓ What products and services will we offer?
✓ To which customers or users?
✓ How will selling/buying decisions be made?
✓ How will we distribute our products and services?
✓ What technologies will we employ?
✓ What capabilities and capacities will we require?
✓ Which capabilities and capacities are core?
✓ What will we make, what will we buy, and what will we acquire through alliance?
✓ What are our options?
✓ On what basis will we compete?

When to Update your Business Strategy

The strategy needs to be frequently reviewed against the prevailing external and internal environment (TOWS analysis). This is where business intelligence comes in, where you need to continually monitor how the strategy and the objectives are being executed. Every 5 to 15 years, most companies suffer from some unexpected misfortune. Indeed, one part of a strategy should be to build in enough buffer or slack to be able to ride out any storm. Be that internal or external.

Many businesses have the strategy but then do little with it, thinking simply because we have one, we can move on! It is essential to come back to your strategy, update it and see what opportunities and learnings you can take.

Checklist to help review your strategy:

1. **Customers** – Invest in getting to know who your existing and ideal customers are. More than ever, you have to cater to them if you want to keep them loyal to your brand. We have a new type of customer today. They are informed. They do their research, so if you do not have a plan to actively retain your customers, they **will** go elsewhere.
2. **Finance** – This is one of the most daunting parts of a company for a leader without accounting or finance expertise; it is also one of the most important. If you are not confident in your skills, find a way to boost them without delay.
   Take a course, find an experienced adviser, or hire someone highly qualified. You have to understand your business's key financial ratios and what your ratios mean within your company. You must understand the components that go into your income statement, balance sheet, and cash flow systems. You can make a significant difference in your business very quickly just by applying a couple of strategies.
3. **Distribution systems** – You must have a plan for getting your product to your customer with the least amount of effort for them and the quickest amount of time. You have got to understand what are the best ways that you can get to your customer.
4. **Marketing** – Gone are the days when basic marketing strategies were all small business owners needed. You have

got to be able to know the exact customer that you have. A lot of successful businesses will take advantage of a niche or very targeted marketing. That way, you can compete with the more prominent companies because you focus on a targeted customer that brings in the most significant return.

5. **Products and services** – Unless you're able to analyse the products and services well – that is, you have a system for doing it–you may not quite realize the types of products and services that will have the most significant impact on your sales.

6. **Pricing strategies** – Know your products and understand their worth to consumers. That means objectively evaluating their quality so you can come up with the best price and selling strategy. Many business owners do not consider pricing strategies as well as they could. Just a simple change in your pricing can make a major impact on your sales and your revenue.

7. **People** – Human resources are among your most valuable. Know your people, and make sure your staff resonate with your organisation's values and vice versa. It is imperative that you have your people on the same page. That they understand what they are doing impacts your business's overall mission. As a business owner, you must understand the drivers of good and poor performance. If you identify employee performance problems early to correct them, it does not affect your business as much.

8. **Performance** – Business owners need to be able to measure their people; they have got to be able to measure their processes, and they have got to be able to measure their system performance. That means having consistent metrics across all parts of your company.

9. **Sales** – You have got to make sure that your salespeople are equipped with the right tools to be the best salespeople they can be. You've got to develop a reliable system for getting appointments. You've got to teach your sales staff

how to overcome resistance. That means you've got to understand all the possible [forms of] resistance you'll probably get with each of your products.

10. **Technology** – Among the most essential aspects are cloud technology, a reliable email program and security protection for your IT content. These are all things that the savvy business owner is looking for. They are looking at tools that can help automate, and they are looking for tools that can help speed up and simplify processes. They are looking for tools that can drive their business success, so that is important.

Business Plan

Build growth into both your vision and business plan

If you are going to dream, then dream big because reaching one horizon always reveals another.

That is why have a VISION and PLANNING exactly how to achieve that vision are critical success factors in turning big dreams into absolute reality.

Daring to dream pays huge dividends.

Planning for growth is vital. Forecasting and planning for growth enable successful entrepreneurs to scale the business up without strangling it or running out of cash. And therein lies the key factor in effective growth management: cash!

Sustainable growth always comes back to the amount of cash that you have available in the business.

Scalability is about the amount of money that you have in the company to invest in that growth. How, when and in what you invest your profits are the core drivers of growth. With scalability, achieving balance is critical.

For example, a sales-generating business may have periods of exceptional growth. What is vital is how that upsurge in growth is handled. Over-investing is a common mistake made to cover growth.

Unfortunately, if a few leaner months follow a period of growth, staff costs may need to be reduced. And what if you have taken on bigger premises to cope with the growth you can no longer afford? Stable and solid growth comes back to the all-important forecasting model and one key question:

What are you doing with your cash, and how are you reinvesting it? Think carefully about this question frequently as your business grows.

Why you need a business plan

A business plan is a written document that describes your business. It covers objectives, strategies, sales, marketing, and financial forecasts.

A business plan helps you to:

- ✓ clarify your business idea
- ✓ spot potential problems
- ✓ set out your goals
- ✓ measure your progress

Top Tip: Be concise
It is important that potential investors can understand what your business is all about from a quick glance at your plan. Make sure you include a summary of your business and how it will make money right from the start and use simple language throughout.

Key principles in your Business Plan

You must ensure that these elements are reflected within your Business Plan.

Be specific – Being specific is just as important as being concise. The details will help you drill down into how you will deliver your plan.

Know your market – A big part of knowing whether your business will be successful is understanding your audience. Make sure your plan is clear about your target market – who will you be selling to, and how many other companies are already selling similar products?

Know your finances – The other essential part of a business plan is the finance section. If your business is not going to make any money, it will not be successful, so you need to be very clear on making a profit. Use it to your advantage – your plan will be beneficial for securing loans and investment, but that is not its only use. It is also a personal tool to help you understand your objectives.

In the next section, we will take a deep dive into the various sections expected to be present in your business plan, and the order you may wish to adopt in presenting them.

However, just before getting to this, we ought to also mention your Business Model!

Business Structure

Far too many business owners get Strategy and Structure the wrong way around. It creates a bottleneck in the business growth which will ultimately become a stranglehold in the business's ability to grow.

It would be best if you start by defining what the business strategy is and then turning to the business's structure and makeup to support the strategy. Get this the wrong way around, and it is the same as trying to build a large block of flats and, once complete, determining the foundations' size and shape!

To define the right structure for your business, first review the various models available to determine which you feel is best to pursue.

Business Model

At its core, your business model is a description of how your business makes money. It is an explanation of how you deliver value to your customers at a reasonable cost.

According to Joan Magretta in "Why Business Models Matter" (Magretta, 2002) the term business model came into wide use with the advent of the personal computer and the spreadsheet.

These tools let entrepreneurs' experiment, test, and model different ways to structure their costs and revenue streams. Spreadsheets allow entrepreneurs to make quick, hypothetical changes to their business model and immediately see how the change might impact their business now and in the future.

In their simplest forms, business models can be broken into three parts:

1. *Everything it takes to make something: design, raw materials, manufacturing, labour, and so on.*
2. *Everything it takes to sell that thing: marketing, distribution, delivering a service, and processing the sale.*
3. *How and what the customer pays: pricing strategy, payment methods, payment timing, etc.*

As you can see, a business model is simply an exploration of what costs and expenses you have and how much you can charge for your product or service.

A successful business model just needs to collect more money from customers than it costs to make the product. This is your profit.

New business models can refine and improve any of these three components.

Maybe you can lower costs during design and manufacturing. Or, perhaps you can find more effective methods of marketing and sales. Or perhaps you can figure out an innovative way for customers to pay.

Keep in mind, though, that you do not have to come up with a new business model to have an effective strategy. Instead, you could take an existing business model and offer it to different customers. For example, restaurants primarily operate on a standard business model but focus their strategy by targeting different kinds of customers.

An example of different kinds of business model

You do not have to invent an entirely new business model to start a business. Most companies use existing business models and refine them to find a competitive edge.

Here is a list of just a few of the most common business models you could apply within your business:

1. Advertising
The advertising business model has been around a long time and has become more sophisticated as the world has transitioned from print to online. The model's fundamentals revolve around creating content that people want to read or watch and then displaying advertising to your readers or viewers.

You must satisfy two customer groups in an advertising business model: your readers or viewers and your advertisers.

Your readers may or may not be paying you, but your advertisers certainly are.

An advertising business model is sometimes combined with a crowdsourcing model where you get your content free from users instead of paying content creators to develop content.

2. Affiliate
The affiliate business model is related to the advertising business model but has some specific differences. The affiliate model most frequently found online uses links embedded in content instead of visual advertisements that are easily identifiable.

For example, if you run a book review website, you could embed affiliate links to Amazon within your reviews that allow people to buy the book you are reviewing. Amazon will pay you a small commission for every sale that you refer to them.

3. Brokerage
Brokerage businesses connect buyers and sellers and help facilitate a transaction.
They charge a fee for each transaction to either the buyer or the seller and sometimes both.

One of the most common brokerage businesses is an estate agency. Still, there are many other types of brokerages, such as freight brokers and brokers who help construction companies find buyers for dirt that they excavate from new foundations.

4. Concierge/customisation
Some businesses take existing products or services and add a custom element to the transaction that makes every sale unique for the given customer.

For example, think of custom travel agents who book trips and experiences for wealthy clients. You can also find customisation happening at a larger scale with products like Nike's custom footwear.

5. Crowdsourcing
If you can bring together many people to contribute content to your site, then you are crowdsourcing. Crowdsourcing business models are most frequently paired with advertising models to generate revenue, but many other iterations of the model.

Companies trying to solve complex problems often publish their issues openly for anyone to solve. Successful solutions get rewards, and the company can then grow their business. The key to a successful crowdsourcing business is providing the right rewards to entice the *"crowd"* while also enabling you to build a viable business.

6. Disintermediation
If you want to make and sell something in stores, you typically work through a series of go-betweens to get your product from the factory to the store shelf.

Disintermediation is when you sidestep everyone in the supply chain and sell directly to consumers, allowing you to potentially lower costs to your customers and have a direct relationship with them as well.

7. Fractionalisation
Instead of selling an entire product, you can sell just part of that product with a fractionalisation business model.

One of the best examples of this business model is timeshares, where a group of people owns only a portion of a holiday home, enabling them to use it for a certain number of weeks every year.

8. Franchise

Franchising is common in the restaurant industry, but you will also find it in all sorts of service industries, from cleaning businesses to staffing agencies.

In a franchise business model, you sell the recipe for starting and running a successful business to someone else. You are often also selling access to a national brand and support services that help the new franchise owner get up and running. In effect, you are selling access to a successful business model that you have developed.

9. Freemium

With a freemium business model, you are giving away part of your product or service for free and charging for premium features or services.

Freemium is not the same as a free trial where customers only get access to a product or service for a limited period. Instead, freemium models allow for unlimited use of essential features for free and only charge customers who want access to more advanced functionality.

10. Leasing

Leasing might seem like fractionalisation, but they are very different. In fractionalisation, you are selling continuous access to part of something.

Leasing, on the other hand, is like renting.

At the end of a lease agreement, a customer needs to return the product they were renting from you.

Leasing is most used for high-priced products where customers may not afford a full purchase but could instead afford to rent the product for a while.

11. Low touch

With a low-touch business model, companies lower their prices by providing fewer services. Some of the best examples of this type of business model are budget airlines and furniture sellers like IKEA. In both cases, the low-touch business model means that customers need to either purchase additional services or do some things themselves to keep costs down.

12. Marketplace

Marketplaces allow sellers to list items for sale and provide customers with easy tools for connecting to sellers.

The marketplace business model can generate revenue from various sources, including fees to the buyer or the seller for a successful transaction, additional services for helping advertise the seller's products, and insurance, so buyers have peace of mind. The marketplace model has been used for both products and services.

13. Pay-as-you-go

Instead of pre-purchasing a certain amount of something, such as electricity or mobile phone minutes, customers get charged for actual usage at the end of a billing period. The pay-as-you-go model is most common for mobile phone, the internet, and some residential energy suppliers, but it has been applied to things like printer ink.

14. Razor blade

The razor blade business model is named after the product that invented the model: sell a durable product below cost to increase volume sales of a high-margin, disposable product component.

Therefore, razor blade companies practically give away the razor handle, assuming that you will continue to buy a large volume of blades over the long term. The goal is to tie a customer into a system, ensuring many additional, ongoing purchases over time.

15. Reverse razor blade

Flipping the razor blade model around, you can offer a high-margin product and promote sales of a low-margin companion product.

Like the razor blade model, customers are often choosing to join an ecosystem of products. Unlike the razor blade model, the initial purchase is the big sale where a company makes most of its money. The add-ons are just there to keep customers using the initially expensive product.

16. Reverse auction

A reverse auction business model turns auctions upside down and has sellers present their lowest prices to buyers. Buyers then have the option to choose the lowest price.

You can see reverse auctions in action when contractors bid to do work on a construction project. You also see reverse auctions anytime you shop for a mortgage or other type of loan.

17. Subscription

Subscription business models are becoming increasingly common. In this business model, consumers get charged a subscription fee to get access to a service.

While magazine and newspaper subscriptions have been around for a long time, the model has now spread to software and online services and is even showing up in service industries.

This is by no means an exhaustive list of all business models that exist—but, hopefully, it gets you thinking about how you might structure your business.

The key thing to remember is that you do not need to invent a new business model when starting your business. Using existing models can help lead you to success because the model has been proven to work. You will be innovating in smaller ways within that existing business model to grow your business.

Business Model Canvas is strategic management and lean start-up template for developing new or documenting existing business models. It is a visual chart with elements describing a firm's or product's value proposition, infrastructure, customers, and finances. It assists firms in aligning their activities by illustrating potential trade-offs.

The following nine "*building blocks*" of the business model design template that came to be called the Business Model Canvas were initially proposed in 2005 by Alexander Osterwalder based on his earlier work on business model ontology (Osterwalder, 2004). Since the release of Osterwalder's creation in 2008, new canvases for specific niches have appeared.

Here, Osterwalder has used descriptions of the business to form the building blocks for its various activities.

A new business model could be highly lucrative but also brings higher risk. You do not know if customers will accept the model or not.

The Business Model Canvas

| Designed for: | Designed by: | Date: | Version: |

KEY PARTNERS

Who are our Key Partners?
Who are our Key Suppliers?
Which Key Resources are we acquiring from partners?
Which Key Activities do partners perform?

MOTIVATIONS FOR PARTNERSHIPS

Optimisation and Economy
Reduction of risk and uncertainty
Acquisition of particular resources and activities

KEY ACTIVITIES

What Key Activities do our Value Propositions require?
Our Distribution Channels?
Customer Relationships?
Revenue Streams?

CATEGORIES

Production
Problem Solving
Platform / Network

KEY RESOURCES

What Key Resources do our Value Proposition require?
Our Distribution Channels?
Customer Relationships?
Revenue Streams?

TYPES OF CATEGORIES

Physical
Intellectual (brand, patents, copyrights, data)
Human
Financial

VALUE PROPOSITIONS

What value do we deliver to the customer?
Which one of our customer's problems are we helping to solve?
What bundles of products and services are we offering each Customer Segment?
Which customer needs satisfying?

CHARACTERISTICS

Newness
Performance
Customisation
"Getting the job done"
Design
Brand / Status
Price
Cost Reduction
Risk Reduction
Accessibility
Convenience / Usability

Channels

Through which Channels do our customer segments want to be reached?
How are we reaching them now?
How are our Channels integrated?
Which ones work best?
Which ones are most cost-efficient?
How are we integrating them with customer routines?

CHANNEL PHASES
Awareness
How do we raise awareness about our company's products and services?
Evaluation
How do we help customers evaluate our oragnisation's Value Proposition?
Purchase
How do we allow customers to purchase specific products and services?
Delivery
How do we deliver a Value Proposition to customers?

Customer segments

For whom are we creating value?
Who are our most important customers?

Mass Market
Niche Market
Segmented
Diversified
Multi-sided Platform

customer relationships

What type of relationship does each of our Customer Segments expect us to establish and maintain with them?
Which one(s) have we established?
How are they integrated with the rest of our business model?
How costly are they?

EXAMPLES

Personal Assistance
Dedicated Personal Assistance
Self Service
Automated Services
Communities
Co-creation

REVENUE STREAMS

For what value are our customers really willing to pay?
For what do they currently pay?
How are they currently paying?
How would they prefer to pay?
How much does each Revenue Stream contribute to overall revenue?

TYPES	DYNAMIC PRICING	FIXED PRICING
Asset Sale	Yield Management	List Price
Usage Fee	Negotiation (bargaining)	Product feature dependant
Subscription Fee		

COST STRUCTURE

What are the most important costs inherent in our business model?
Which Key Resources are most expensive?
Which Key Activities are most expensive?

IS YOUR BUSINESS MORE

Cost Driven (leanest cost structure, low price value proposition, maximum automation, extensive outsourcing)

SAMPLE CHARACTERISTICS

Fixed Costs (salaries, rent, utilities)
Variable Costs

Business Plan - Getting started

Whose plan is this?

Business and owner details:

Business name:

Owner(s) name:

Business address and postcode:

Business telephone number:

Business email address:

Home address and postcode (if different from above):

Home telephone number (if different from above):

Home email address (if different from above):

1. Executive Summary

1.1 Business summary

1.2 Business aims

1.3 Financial summary

1.4 Elevator Pitch

1.5 Your business name

1.6 Strapline

2. Owner's Background

2.1 Why do you want to run your own business?

2.2 Previous work experience

2.3 Qualifications and education

2.4 Training

2.4.1   Details of future training courses you wish to

complete:

2.5 Hobbies and interests

3. Products and Services

3.1 What are you going to sell?

3.1.1   a product

3.1.2   a service

3.1.3   both

3.2 Describe the primary product/service you are going to sell.

3.3 Describe the different types of product/service you are going to be selling.

3.4 If you are not going to sell all your products/services at the start of your business, explain why not and when you will start selling them.

4. The Market

4.1 Are your customers:

4.1.1   Individuals?

4.1.2   Businesses?

4.1.3   Both?

4.2 Describe your typical customer.

4.3 Where are your customers based?

4.4 What prompts your customers to buy your product/service?

4.5 What factors help your customers choose which company to buy from?

4.6 Have you sold products/services to customers already?

4.6.1   yes

4.6.2   no

4.6.3   If you answered "yes", give details:

4.7 Have you got customers waiting to buy your product/service?

4.7.1   yes

4.7.2   no

4.7.3   If you answered "yes", give details:

5. Market Research

5.1 Key findings from desk research

5.2 Key findings from field research – customer questionnaires

5.3 Key findings from field research – test trading

5.4 Additional information:

6. Marketing Strategy

6.1 What are you going to do?

6.2 Why have you chosen this marketing method?

6.3 How much will it cost?

6.4 TOTAL COST

7. Competitor Analysis

7.1 Table of competitors

7.1.1   Name, location

7.1.2   Business size

7.1.3   Product/Service

7.1.4   Price

7.2 TOWS analysis

7.2.1   Threats

7.2.2   Opportunities

7.2.3   Weaknesses

7.2.4   Strengths

7.3 Unique Selling Proposition (USP)

8. Operations and Logistics

8.1 Production

8.2 Delivery to customers

8.3 Payment methods and terms

8.4 Suppliers

8.4.1   Name and location of the supplier

8.4.2   Items required and prices

8.4.3   Payment arrangements

8.4.4   Reasons for choosing a supplier

8.5 Premises:

8.6 Equipment

8.6.1   If being bought

8.6.2   Item required

8.6.3   Already owned?

8.6.4   New or second hand?

8.6.5   Purchased from

8.6.6   Price

8.7 Transport:

8.8 Legal requirements:

8.9 Insurance requirements:

8.10   Management and staff

9. Costs and Pricing Strategy

9.1 Number of units in the calculation

9.1.1 Product/service component

9.2 Components cost.

9.3 Total product/service cost

9.3.1 Cost per unit

9.3.2 Price per unit

9.3.3 Profit margin (£)

9.3.4 Profit margin (%)

9.3.5 Mark up (%)

10. Financial Forecasts

10.1　　　Sales and costs forecast.

Month	Sales	Costs	Profit
1			
2			
3			
4			
5			
6			
7			
8			
9			
10			
11			
12			

10.2　　　Total

10.3　　　Assumptions (e.g. Seasonal trends)

10.4　　　Income/Expenses

11. Back-up Plan

11.1   Short-term plan

11.2   Long-term plan

11.3   (Alternate Markets)

Strategy & Structure: Conclusion

Having established what YOU want to achieve (within Chapter 1), it is just as essential to ensure the business is built in a manner capable of delivering this to you. As you can well appreciate, whilst St Paul's Cathedral and The Shard are both large buildings, the footprint of both is as significant as their foundations!

Likewise, what you wish to build determines the foundations, the materials, and the method of successfully and sustainably building it.

Once this has been determined and established, your business plan then enables you to plan the road map for delivering on this. Only then can we turn our attention to customers, determine whom we want to work with and how we will attract them!

Further reading

For more information and a deeper dive into this, there are a couple of great books I can recommend:
Good Strategy Bad Strategy: *The Difference and Why It Matters (Richard P. Rumelt)*

Another great read would be **The Decision Book***:*
50 models for strategic thinking (Roman Tschappeler)

Chapter Four:

Marketing Management

You will note from the title. It does NOT only say Marketing. It reads Marketing MANAGEMENT.

> *"Half the money I spend on advertising is wasted;*
> *the trouble is, I don't know which half."*
> **John Wanamaker**

That may have been accepted as an excuse around 1915 when John Wanamaker (owner of a chain of US department stores) first made it. But it simply does not wash any longer.

With the ability to track, monitor, review, and consider EVERY aspect of EVERY interaction with another human being. Be it an enquiry, a prospect, a customer, supplier or competitor. There is every reason why your marketing should be a profitable segment of the business, and not, as so many currently do, leave it to chance.

However, we also need to burst a long-held and unfounded myth, best described by Mathew Kimberley's quote in his book "Get a grip."

> *"Marketing doesn't get you business,*
> *Marketing gets you awareness.*
> *It is what you do with the awareness*
> *that gets you the business."*

Now we have dispelled that myth. Perhaps it is time to turn our attention to effective Marketing Management.

The 'Triple M' of Effective Marketing

1. Market
2. Message
3. Media

In that order.

I cannot tell you the number of business owners who decide they will "boost a post" or pay for some form of social media adverting to attract new business!

Or perhaps you are one of the "lucky" ones to receive that phone call from a national newspaper, mid-morning on a Friday to be advised:

> *We have some last-minute advertising space in our weekend business supplement read by over 100,000 business owners. And if you can get your advertising 'copy' submitted and approved by 3 pm this afternoon, we will not charge you the usual £10,000 that others have paid to advertise, but just £2,500!*

Your heart is racing as you rush to get a compelling advert together before the deadline and nervously but excitedly offer your credit card details. Knowing full well the number of new orders this advert will generate is going to cover your credit card bill before it is due for payment!

Right?

WRONG. If THIS is your marketing management, you are likely to get a better return by stepping out of the door of your office and gifting £10,000 to the nearest passer-by, with the hope they may show pity on you and spend some of it; buying from your business! Seriously, this is NOT good marketing management.

You must start with Your IDEAL target market, your ideal customer *'avatar'*. Only once you have a good idea about who they are can you begin to determine your message – What do they want/need to hear/ see/feel to build a Know, Like, and Trust relationship with you, your business, and your brand.

Then it is time to tie the two together and establish – Where, When, and How do I get my message in front of my Ideal Target Audience. At the right time, in the right way to influence them sufficiently, WHEN they have made a buying decision, they choose to purchase from me and not my competition?

Your Customer Avatar

Niche marketing is defined as channelling all marketing efforts towards one well-defined segment of the population.

It is a marketing tactic deployed to target a specific and unique market segment. It is often created by identifying what a customer wants. This can be done if the company knows what the customer needs and then delivers a better solution to a problem they face. A niche market does not mean a small market, but it involves a specific target audience with a specialized offering. By doing so, the company becomes a market leader, and it becomes possible for other firms to enter that segment.

For example, if I were to ask 100 people how much they would pay to have their car valeted, there would be a myriad of answers. Ranging from 0 (they do it themselves or wouldn't consider having it done) to maybe a couple of hundred pounds (if it was their pride and joy and was either being used for a special occasion or being prepared for sale). However, for one company initially based in Halifax, West Yorkshire (United Kingdom), they have taken car valeting and paint protection to an entirely new level. At the time of publishing, their price list STARTS at £8,000 and quickly travels north!

However, not to be outdone, Scotland-based Ultimate Shine is recorded as *"The world's most expensive car wash"* charging a whooping £100,000 for its most premium package!

There are various advantages of niche marketing. One of the benefits of a niche market is that there is little or no competition within that segment. The company is virtually the market leader and enjoys a price monopoly. Another benefit is the strong relationship with the customers because the company operates in a small segment. The relationship between the company and the brand becomes more robust, which is also a key to customer loyalty. Niche businesses are often high margin businesses. Customers do not mind paying a little extra because they can only get that service in that company or under its brand.

What is Customer Avatar?

A customer avatar is a detailed profile of your ideal customer. It does not make assumptions or categorise people into groups. The avatar focuses on one person and outlines everything about them. It goes into much greater depth than a regular marketing persona, providing marketers with many more targeting tools.

It is crucial that you create a customer avatar of your ideal customer, not your average buyer.

Your perfect customer is somebody you really want to sell to. They are high-spending, loyal, repeat buying, referral monsters.

Who Needs a Customer Avatar?

Short answer: every business!

Long answer: Small and medium-sized businesses will benefit most from having their customer avatar(s).

Brands of this size need to ensure that the most are made from their staff's time and marketing budgets. A customer avatar allows them to do both things, instantly targeting the business's ideal customer.

Businesses who have previously spent tons of time, effort and money without ever making a decent ROI will also massively benefit from a detailed customer avatar.

Why You Need a Customer Avatar

One of the most common marketing errors made in digital marketing is broad targeting. This usually results in one of the following problems:

1. Brands and businesses that try to appeal to everyone end up appealing to nobody.
2. Marketers who try to speak everyone's language connect with nobody.
3. Businesses who attempt to reach everyone spend way over the odds and (rarely) reach their target market (especially their ideal customer).

It is crucial that you KNOW your target market.

The better you know your target market, the more people you will connect with, the more repeat buyers you will create, and the more referrals you will generate...

...and all of this will come at a much smaller cost!

A detailed customer avatar will also streamline your business at every level. When you have an avatar in your crosshairs, everybody involved in the company can up their game and focus their efforts efficiently.

Product Development
You will be able to create a product/service that is specifically aimed at one person. This makes the process more personalised,

targeted, and relevant. Products/Services like this will resonate instantly with your ideal customer.

Content Marketing

A customer avatar uncovers your ideal customer's real pain points, allowing content creators to produce content that solves and appeals to their needs. This type of content is evergreen, does very well on search engines and engages with your actual target market. If you can solve your customer's real pain points, your brand will be much more appealing.

Paid Traffic

If you are running ads, it is imperative that you have an exact customer avatar in mind. When time and money are involved, you must give your ads every opportunity to perform at their optimum. Understanding everything about your ideal customer allows you to target them precisely, hone your creative and write your copy effectively.

User Experience

When you know who your ideal customer is, you can create the perfect experience for them, beginning with their first interaction, web visit and purchase. A perfect user experience guarantees repeat custom and referrals.

How to Create a Customer Avatar

Now you know how valuable a customer avatar is, it is time to create one. You will need to start by drawing up a long list of questions and getting inside your ideal customer's head before answering them as accurately as possible.

What questions should you ask?

Everything and anything! The more you know about your ideal customer, the better you will be able to target them.

What to Include

There are five major components to the customer avatar. You will need to survey or have conversations with existing customers to flesh out your avatar accurately. In other cases, you will be intimately familiar with the characteristics of your ideal customer.

In any case, move forward. Do not wait for surveys or interviews to be conducted to create your first draft of an avatar. Make assumptions where you have no data or feedback and put it on your shortlist of to-dos to complete your research.

In the meantime, you will begin getting benefit from an avatar built from the assumptions you have made.

Goals and Values
Begin with the goals and values of your ideal customer.

Make a note of the goals and values that are relevant to the products and services you offer. You will use this information to drive: Product/Service creation, Copywriting, Content Marketing, and Email marketing.

> *My ideal customer would read [BOOK], Subscribes to [MAGAZINE], but no one else.*
>
> *They attend [CONFERENCE]. They drive a [CAR], live in [POSTCODE], be aged between [LOWER AGE – UPPER AGE] and have [CHILDREN/PETS].*

Sources of Information
You will determine the best places to advertise and the targeting options you will use to reach your avatar by listing where they get their information sources.

Are you getting the picture?

The idea is to find niche books, magazines, blogs, conferences, gurus, etc. Your ideal customer would be attracted to and learn

135

more about them as a person instead of just knowing what their current problem is that you are aiming to solve.

Demographic Information
Applying demographic information will bring your customer avatar to life.

The usual demographics are critical as they are beneficial to "get inside the head" of your ideal customer.

They are another valuable part of the Customer Avatar when choosing targeting options in ad platforms like Facebook.

When writing content, email, or sales copy, it can be beneficial to simply write as though your avatar is sitting across the table from you. Demographic information like age, gender, and location will give your persona a look and feel.

Challenges and Pain Points
This will drive new product/service development and the copywriting and ad creative you will use to compel your ideal customer to action.

Objections and Role in Purchase Process
Why would your customer avatar choose NOT to buy your product or service?

These are called "objections", and they must be addressed in your marketing.

You must also determine your avatar's role in the purchasing process.

- ✓ Are they the primary decision maker?
- ✓ Are they a decision influencer?

Understanding your ideal customers' decision-making process is paramount to the success of your marketing and sales campaigns.

Build Multiple Avatars
Start by building a single avatar. But do not stop there.

Once you get the hang of it, you will be churning out multiple avatars representing your market's different segments. Do not go overboard, but any lucrative market segment with a distinct set of goals, sources of information, pain points, etc., is deserving of a customer avatar.

When you have your customer avatar template ready, it is time to begin.

As a rule of thumb, I always start by giving them a name. This makes your customer avatar easy to remember, reference and helps you flesh out an artificial character. After coming up with a name, continue through age, gender, marital status, number/age of children, location, occupation, job title etc.

It is crucial that you are super-specific from start to finish. For example, when entering 'age', do not write 30-40. Being broad is exactly what you are trying to avoid! Be specific. Get to know this 'avatar' as if they are a real person.

If you want, you can even find a photo of somebody who represents your ideal customer.

When all the general information is complete, move on to 'goals and values.

As you enter the information, make sure you never veer from your customer avatar's mindset. It is very easy to slip into your own or that of your average buyer. Be them for twenty minutes. You will learn a lot.

Conclusion

A customer avatar should be a fundamental element of your marketing strategy. It creates a foundation for targeting and allows everyone in your business to understand exactly who you are striving to attract.

Marketing campaigns that already know their target market's specifics will always require less money and time and provide a greater ROI.

Lead Magnets

Before we get into lead magnets, let us confirm what a lead is.

Typically, this is a potential customer for your business. They might buy from you. But you want them to definitely buy from you! So, you need to make sure that the leads you attract are the right ones. To understand who your potential customers are, you need to do a bit of research. Start with your existing customer base and profile them. The better picture you can get of who buys from you, the better you can target your marketing to find new people just like them.

It is simply a piece of content that draws the type of leads you want to your business. It is a way for you to identify potential customers.

A lead magnet can come in different forms:

- ✓ A PDF Report/Whitepaper
- ✓ An eBook
- ✓ A video
- ✓ A webinar

These are just a few of the many lead magnets out there, but these are the most popular digital lead magnets. What these different formats have in common when used as a lead magnet, is value.

What you offer should be valuable enough for a person to want it badly enough that they will give you their details in return.

This is all part of the Know, LOVE and Trust part of the courtship. It's all about building a positive **emotional** bank balance. Therefore, the more you give, and the less you ask for, the more positive an emotional bank balance you are left with.

That means no selling!

What you put in a lead magnet needs to be informative and solve your target audience's problems. When you put together your lead magnet, think about your audience's pain points and ask yourself if you solve them. If you can say 'Yes', then you have yourself a great lead magnet.

Why do you need a lead magnet?
The main reason to use lead magnets is to grow your database of potential customers. Once a person has permitted you to contact them (an 'opt-in' to be included with the digital offering delivery), you can then continue to build a relationship with them.

If I had a pound for every small business owner who tells me social media is how to get new customers, I would be on yet another very luxurious holiday right now!

What you need to remember is that you do not own the social network you use. It could disappear tomorrow, taking your audience with it. More likely still, the algorithm will change (just when you thought you had worked it out) and your engagement will drop.

A database list is yours. You have more control over whether your content gets seen or not. Therefore, focusing on growing your database will give you a ready-made pool of potential customers. Think about it: when you have a new product or service to promote, your list will be ready to hear about it. They know you, like you and trust you. So, it stands to reason that they will be more likely to buy from you.

Did you forget something?...

Just because you built it, does not mean they will come! You must promote the lead magnet across all the forms of media you have identified that your Avatar uses so that they become aware of the opportunity and respond. Your lead magnet's success shall be determined by your ability to connect with your ideal target audience in such a manner that to do so is a 'no brainer'.

Customer Relationship Management

A Customer Relationship Management (CRM) system helps manage customer data. It supports sales management, delivers actionable insights, integrates with social media, and facilitates team communication.

Cloud-based CRM systems offer complete mobility and access to a myriad of bespoke apps.

A CRM system helps businesses keep customer contact details up to date, tracks every customer interaction, and manages customer accounts. It is designed to help companies to improve customer relationships and Customer Lifetime Value. This is vital because of the vast amount of such data businesses generate daily.

The issue of customer data raises a challenge that CRM systems exist to address. Every time someone picks up the phone and talks to a customer goes out to meet a new sales prospect, or follows up a promising lead, they learn something new and potentially valuable. Traditionally, all this data went into analogue or unconnected media such as notebooks or laptops, or even just stayed in people's heads.

Without a CRM, these methods make it all too easy for details to get lost or forgotten. For a meeting or phone conversation not to be followed up on as promised. Choosing which leads or prospects to focus on can be a matter of guesswork rather than a rigorous exercise based on fact.

Worse still, if the person holding access to crucial customer information were to leave, then all their knowledge could walk out of the door with them.

Which CRM is right for you?

A CRM system helps ensure accuracy and efficiency. It takes customer data and turns it into useful, actionable insight that can transform a business. It helps everyone in a business to update records easily and to get access to the latest information. If the system is cloud-based, they can do this wherever they are, on any connected device.

However, with so many different CRM's available, it can be just as difficult to determine which is right for you and your business.

For me, the answer becomes far easier. As previously stated, – start with the end in mind!

Think of your successful business in 5, 6, maybe even ten years. Consider how big it will be and how many customers it will serve. How many different products/services will it be providing? Now, look at which of the many CRM's you think are best to service that size of business. Which ones appear forward-thinking, have regular updates and a vision statement that meets you and your growing businesses requirements?

Your CRM is likely to become the 'engine room' for the leads, conversions, and management of customers' data within your business. Therefore, it is vital to get the right 'engine' to do the job.

My suggestion of starting with the end in mind and working backwards is purely one to prevent difficulty and distress later in the business.

Setting up a new CRM can be daunting. However, this is nothing against moving from one system to another once you have everything set up and working for you with an existing CRM!

Analytics

It is crucial that you have useful analytics embedded within your website and monitor results (at least monthly).

What gets measured gets managed.

Web analytics is the measurement, collection, analysis, and reporting of web data to understand and optimise web usage. However, web analytics is not just a process for measuring web traffic. It can also be used as a tool for business and market research and assess and improve a website's effectiveness.

Web analytics applications can also help measure the results of traditional print or broadcast advertising campaigns. It helps to estimate how traffic to your website changes after the launch of a new advertising campaign. It provides information about the number of visitors to a website and the number of page views. It also helps gauge traffic and popularity trends, which is helpful for market research.

Branding

Another crucial element of your marketing campaign is that you have a strong brand image that runs continually through all your marketing (both online and offline).

What is Branding, and why is it important to business?
By definition, branding is a marketing practice in which a company creates a name, symbol or design that is easily identifiable as belonging to the company. And whilst this is

fundamentally true, branding is so much more than simply a name, a symbol, or a design.

Branding helps to identify a product and distinguish it from other products and services. It is essential because not only is it what makes a memorable impression on consumers, but it allows your customers and clients to know what to expect from your company. It is a way of distinguishing yourself from the competitors and clarifying what you offer that makes you the better choice.

Your brand is built to be an accurate representation of who you are as a business and how you wish to be perceived.

Many areas are used to develop a brand, including advertising, customer service, promotional merchandise, reputation, and logo. All these elements work together to create one unique and attention-grabbing professional profile.

Why Is Branding Important?

Branding is critical to a business because of the overall impact it makes on your company. Branding can change how people perceive your brand; it can drive new business and increase brand awareness.

Branding gets recognition
The most crucial reason branding is vital to a business is how a company gets recognition and becomes known to the consumers.

Branding increases business value
Branding is essential when generating future business, and a firmly established brand can increase a business' value by giving the company more leverage in the industry. This makes it a more attractive investment opportunity because of its firmly established place in the marketplace.

Branding generates new customers

A good brand will have no trouble drumming up referral business. Strong branding generally means there is a positive impression of the company amongst consumers. They are likely to do business with you because of the familiarity and assumed dependability of using a name they can trust. Once a brand has been well-established, word of mouth will be the company's best and most effective advertising technique.

Improves employee pride and job satisfaction

When an employee works for a strongly branded company and truly stands behind the brand, they are more likely to be satisfied with their job and have a higher degree of pride in their work. Working for a reputable brand and held in high regard amongst the public makes working for that company more enjoyable and fulfilling. Having a branded office, which can often help employees feel more satisfied and have a sense of belonging to the company, can be achieved using promotional merchandise.

Creates trust within the marketplace

A professional appearance and well thought through branding strategy will help the company build trust with consumers, potential clients, and customers. People are more likely to do business with a company that has a professional portrayal. Being properly branded gives the impression of being industry experts and makes the public feel as though they can trust your company, the products and services it offers and the way it handles its business.

Branding Supports Advertising

Advertising is another component of branding, and advertising strategies will directly reflect the brand and its desired portrayal. Advertising techniques such as promotional products from trusted companies that provide outstanding branding make it easy to create a cohesive and appealing advertising strategy that plays well into your branding goals.

Newsletter

You should aim to run a newsletter (at least monthly), giving value to your list(s).

A newsletter keeps your organisation fresh in the customer's mind. As every business owner knows, it is a lot easier to nurture existing customer relationships than to establish new relationships.
That is because your current customers already know and trust you. Newsletters are a fantastic tool to help reinforce these valuable relationships.

Promote without Selling

The purpose of a newsletter is simple: to inform and update customers about recent happenings within your company and industry. Every business has exciting and beneficial information to share with customers. For instance, did you add a new product/service or receive some noteworthy recognition? Are there any important events, trends, or recommendations you want to share?

By increasing awareness through a regular newsletter, you reinforce your firm's credibility and remain continually fresh in your customers' minds. A newsletter helps promote your company subtly and systematically. Bear in mind that it does not serve the same function as a brochure, so it is not the place for flashy advertising or sales hype. Instead, draw attention by providing engaging and useful content that benefits your customers.

The Permanence of Print

Newsletters sent by email are very common, but many businesses wisely still prefer to distribute a printed copy. A printed copy has several advantages over its electronic cousin. A printed copy is portable, so it can be read anywhere and is quickly passed along. It also arrives as a highly visible piece, not as a single line on a cluttered screen that could be easily overlooked, deleted, or diverted as spam.

And because it exists in physical form, a printed newsletter is not quickly discarded.

Printed newsletters tend to linger around a while, which can set your organisation apart – and increases the chance of sparking your customer's memory with a colourful heading or catchy title.

Printed newsletters also exhibit permanence, stability, and trust (after all, how many scammers or fly-by-night companies distribute printed newsletters?)

Simple to Design

Since a newsletter is viewed more as a publication instead of as a promotional piece, it usually has more straightforward design elements than a brochure or catalogue. And because you are relaying concise bits of information, the content is generally straightforward to write. For example, you can provide short profiles of customers, employees, executives, or projects. Or highlight a specific product or industry developments and statistics. Testimonials, FAQs or *"Did You Know*?" sections also provide good newsletter content. Any knowledge that benefits the customer is a high-quality topic.

A newsletter does not need to be lengthy, but it should be distributed at regular intervals, such as monthly or quarterly. To maintain a fresh yet enduring presence, it is better to send out less information more frequently than more information less frequently. It is also essential to have a consistent look among all your newsletters, so the recipients immediately recognize the sender (you!).

Also, imagery is strongly recommended because it provides more illustrative content and prevents otherwise plain text blocks, decreasing readership. Full colour is ideal, but more straightforward colour variations and even grayscale can make images and designs look more appealing. Most newsletters can also be designed as self-mailers to streamline their distribution.

Competition between Print and Digital

For every 16 pieces of print received, your customer will receive 100 emails on average. What is more important, though, is the level of engagement:

Print Direct Mail – 70% opened, and 79% is read for at least 1 minute.

Email – according to Mailchimp, average open rates across different industries varies from 15.22% to 27.23%, with a click-through rate of 1.25% to 5.19%

Printed material is far more engaging and can drive people offline to online or act offline or go to a retail store.

Life of the Email

An email's life is seconds at best and rarely more than 1 minute. Try the following experiment: spend 2 seconds looking at something you have not seen before and then try and recall it 20 mins later. Unless there were something very relevant or interesting, most of us would not be able to remember it, and, if it were of interest, we would have spent more time on it.

7 Reasons to use the Printed Newsletter

1. There is nowhere near the competition for your prospect's attention compared to email.
2. Improved trust makes your company appear more real because they have something physically real in their hands.
3. Lasts longer – it is placed on a desk to be read later or after being read, and others see it. It can be taken from job to job. More time is given, which means your brand now occupies a stronger position in your prospects mind.
4. Better at reaching high-level decision-makers.
5. Will not get stopped by a spam filter.
6. Does not require opt-in.
7. Not everyone is online or easily targeted online.

Marketing Management: Conclusion

Start with the end in mind! Determine what a successful marketing department within your business looks like. Take time to consider whom you want to work with (and whom you don't), the type and style of business you want to do, and who will be most attracted to that?

Consider what they need to see, hear, feel, smell, and taste to determine that you are the right solution for them, beyond any other, and then establish how to bring your message in front of this audience effectively. Only when you take the time to really understand who your customer is and why they buy from you can you effectively manage your marketing, and not be managed by it.

Further reading:

I love the work of Daniel Priestley, in particular the most recent re-write of: Oversubscribed - How to Get People Lining Up to Do Business with You - Don't fight for customers, let them fight over you!

Another GREAT read is Category of One (Joe Calloway) How Extraordinary Companies Transcend Commodity and Defy Comparison.

Chapter Five:

Money and Margins

One of the biggest causes of failure, particularly in smaller businesses, is not fully understanding the difference between the money we make and the cost of making it.

From Micro start-ups to giant international corporations, businesses of all shapes and sizes still make the error of determining a business's success by its turnover!

Turnover is nothing but a vanity matrix. It does not matter. It makes NO difference as to whether the business will be a huge success or another terrible failure. What matters is the DIFFERENCE between how much money it makes and how much it costs to make it!

Money

The business of business is business.

It might appear relatively self-explanatory that it has to be and remain profitable for a business to succeed. Yes, you could argue that some of the largest brands of today have traded for a long time, losing money. However, that is only on the proviso; there has been a significant financial investor willing to absorb those losses (for a whole range of tax efficiency purposes) as a long term strategy knowing (or at least expecting) for it to 'break even' at some stage in the future and sell for an exorbitant amount of money in the future!

However, back in the realms of reality and the more common business approach, there is a need to make money for the business not to go or GROW broke (more on this within the chapter).

Perhaps it may be beneficial if we start by identifying the key numbers you need to know within a business and ensuring some understanding of standard financial terms, their importance, and their relevance to day-to-day business?

Essential Key Business Numbers

28% of businesses fail due to problems with the financial structure of the company. This includes keeping poor accounting records.

Suppose you don't understand your key financial metrics. In that case, you have no way of monitoring your business's health— and you risk mingling assets, incurring penalties for filing taxes late, overlooking expenses, and running into difficulties paying bills and employees, just to mention a few!

Therefore, it is essential to understand what each of these key metrics can tell you about your business's health and monitor how these metrics are performing on an ongoing basis. This will enable you to make better decisions, as well as plan proactively for the future.

Depending on the type of business you operate, the metrics you monitor will differ. For example, if you have an e-commerce website, you will want to measure unique visitors, referrals, bounce rate, and similar. If you are running a subscription business, you will want to track churn rate, monthly recurring revenue, lifetime value, and so on.

However, there are several metrics that every business owner should know, including cash flow, accounts payable, accounts receivable, direct costs, operating margin, net profit, and cash burn rate.

What is Cash Flow?

Cash flow measures the money—the actual pounds, dollar pesos or yen—that is moving in and out of your bank accounts. Cash that you pay out is negative cash flow, and money that comes into your business is positive cash flow. The most important thing to know about cash flow is that it is not profits.

What Is Accounts Payable?

Accounts payable is the total of the bills you must pay, but you have not paid yet. This is a business's short-term debt that must be paid. In your company's financial statements, accounts payable will show up on your balance sheet as a liability. It is essential to track this metric so that you can manage your cash flow. After all, if you cannot control your debts, you could risk defaulting.

What Is Accounts Receivable?

Accounts receivable is owed to you by your customers for products or services you have sold. Because this metric shows as an asset on your financial statements, it is imperative to be aware of it. Remember, this is not money in the bank but the money that is owed to your business.

Encouraging customers to pay invoices faster will decrease your chance of getting into a "cash crunch".

What Are Direct Costs?

Direct costs—also known as *"costs of goods sold"*—are the costs that can be attributed entirely to the production of a specific product or service. These costs include the cost of materials used to create the product and potentially any labour costs that are exclusively used to make it. Direct costs always exclude indirect expenses such as marketing expenses, rent, insurance and so on. Direct costs show up on the Profit and Loss Statement and can be subtracted from revenue to calculate a company's gross margin.

What Is Operating Margin?

Operating margin shows you how good your company is at generating income from normal business operations after you have spent money on marketing, sales, product development, and so on.

What Is Net Profit?

Net profit is your operating income minus taxes and interest. It is the proverbial bottom line of your business; the money you make does not go back into expenses, taxes, and interest—the net profit left over.

What Is Cash Burn Rate?

Cash burn rate is the rate at which a company uses up its cash reserves or cash balance. This metric is designed to show you how fast you are burning through your cash reserves or how you are maintaining a healthy balance from positive cash flow.

Knowing how you are performing allows you to take action that is important to continued growth and even your business's survival.

Suppose you are looking for tools to help you easily keep track of your essential financial metrics.
In that case, you can use an accounting solution like QuickBooks or Xero, or a business management dashboard like LivePlan. The latter will give you instant insight into each of these key metrics and make it easy to compare data from previous periods.

Now, let us take a brief look at just a few of these and look at easy means to try and influence them to our favour.

Cash Flow

To state the obvious, cash is critical to running a business. Without money in your bank account, you cannot pay your bills, buy more inventory, or expand your business.

You can always look at your bank account balance to see how much cash you have at any given time. But, that one number from your bank doesn't tell you much about how money is moving in and out of your account or help you see a projection of how your bank account might look in one month or six months.

That is where cash flow comes in. Cash flow is the measure of how much cash is moving in or out of your business in each period. For example, for one month, you might pay £5,000 in bills and receive £8,000 in cash from your customers. In this case, your total cash flow would be £3,000.

Cash flow calculations are simple:

Cash Received – Cash Paid Out = Cash Flow

In some months, you may have negative cash flow. Do not worry; this is common during slower seasons for some businesses. It is also common as you are growing your business. You may be investing in growth, knowing that sales will come later.

The key to staying in business is that you cannot run out of cash. Banks do not like it when you bounce checks! So, if you have money from investors to grow your business, you may be able to support negative cash flow for some time while you grow your business. Many companies also call this burn rate.

The difference between cash flow and profits

The most important thing to know about cash flow is that it is not profits. Profits and cash are not the same things.

Here is a quick explanation:

When you sell a product to a customer and send that customer an invoice, you often do not get paid right away. Instead, you get paid in 30 days, maybe more. However, when you make this sale, you will show that sale on your Profit and Loss Statement, which will help you calculate profits.

But this sale will not show up in your cash flow until you get the money from your customer. You track sales that you have made but have not been paid for yet in your Accounts Receivable.

Why is cash flow important?

At the most basic level, you need to understand and analyse your cash flow to know if your business bank accounts are growing or shrinking over time. After all, you cannot run out of cash. If you do, you are heading for bankruptcy.

Forecasting your cash flow is critical for anyone running a business. You'll want to know how much cash you need to keep on hand to pay your bills when the best time is to buy new equipment, when you should buy more inventory, and so that you can see how fast growth can hurt your cash position.

That's right; fast growth can put your business in a challenging cash situation. That seems odd, but it's true—especially for businesses that invoice their customers and get paid after delivering their products.

So, how does this happen? Think about a business that sells widgets. To sell the widgets, the company needs to buy the widgets' materials, pay employees to put the widgets together, package them, and finally ship them to the customer.

This business has paid for the widgets, paid salaries, and even paid shipping at this point, but the customer has not paid yet. Since the customer's invoice says "net-30" on the top of it, the customer might take up to 30 days to pay the bill. The business has paid out cash to deliver their widgets but will not receive cash payments until much later.

If your business is growing and large orders are coming in quickly, you will most likely need to have a significant amount of cash in your bank accounts to support this growth.

What is better? Positive or negative cash flow?

Positive cash flow is almost always better. This means that you are bringing money in the doors and accumulating cash to later invest in the business. However, there are cases where a business may be expected to have a negative cash flow. New start-up companies and companies that are investing heavily in growth will often have negative cash flow.

Start-ups need to build their products, invest in initial marketing, and pay salaries before the first customer payments start rolling in. Companies investing in growth might have negative cash flow as they buy new equipment or expand their operations. These companies are hoping that their investment will pay off with more customers and more cash coming into the business over the long term.

How to improve your cash flow

There are many ways to improve your cash flow; I will cover a few of them here.

Get your customers to pay you faster.
The faster your customers pay you, the quicker you get cash in the bank. I cover a few ways to get customers to pay you more quickly later in this chapter on accounts receivable.

Pay your bills a little slower
Sometimes you do not have to pay all your bills right away. The longer you can hold on to your cash, the better the cash position you will have. However, I am NOT advocating failing to pay bills, and there is sometimes an option to negotiate bills based on payment terms (i.e. getting a reduction to pay early). For more on this, see accounts payable later in this chapter.

Get a line of credit
If your business regularly goes through a cash crunch and a period of negative cash flow, you may want to consider a line of credit for your business.

This is a short-term loan that you can draw from as you need it. Many companies use lines of credit to help them through periods of low cash.

Purchase less inventory
Some businesses make the mistake of buying too much inventory. All that inventory can tie up a lot of cash. Instead, see if it makes sense for your business to carry less stock on hand and only order inventory when needed.

Conclusion

Of all metrics in your business, cash flow is almost certainly the most critical number to watch. Cash is the lifeblood of all companies and is necessary for business survival. Understanding whether you are losing cash or piling it up is critical to understanding your business's health.

Beyond just keeping an eye on your cash flow, consider creating a cash flow forecast so you can predict when you might run low on cash and when you should expand.

Accounts Payable

Accounts payable is the total of the bills you must pay, but you haven't paid yet. This is a business's short-term debt that must be paid.

When your business gets a bill in the mail, what happens? Do you pay it immediately, or do you maybe hold onto that bill for a little while before you pay it?

If you run your business like I run mine, you probably hold on to that bill and pay it toward the end of the month. Or, maybe you have a regular day each month where you spend all your bills.

Sometimes—and this is perfectly normal—you might even delay payment on a bill while you wait for your customers to pay you. Like most businesses, you might have more cash to pay bills at certain times of the month and less flexibility at other times. If this sounds like you, do not worry too much—you are not alone!

All those unpaid bills have a name—accounts payable, also known as "*AP*". Accounts payable is the amount of money that you owe to your vendors and suppliers. It is essentially a total of all the invoices you have received but have not paid yet.

In your company's financial statements, accounts payable will show up on your balance sheet as a liability.

Ideally, you should keep your business's financial books organised and enter your bills into your accounting system as they arrive. This does not mean you have to pay your bills right away, but it helps you keep track of whom you owe and what your liabilities are.

You can also get reports from your accounting system (or in LivePlan if you use the Scoreboard feature) that tell you the average amount of time it takes you to pay your bills—AP Days—and which vendors you typically wait for the longest to pay.

Why is accounts payable important?

Tracking your accounts payable is a critical component to managing your cash flow. As your business grows, you may be spending money on different services for your business, and you will receive invoices that need to get paid. If you cannot manage your debts, you could find yourself in a cash crunch, or worse, defaulting on a debt.

Specifically, when you are growing quickly, you may need to buy more inventory and invest in business expansion faster than your customers are paying you. This means that you will have bills that come due before you receive money from your customers.

To stay on top of a situation like this, you need to keep track of your accounts payable and make sure that you have enough cash on hand to continue paying your bills. Ideally, you should forecast your growth and make sure that you plan to have enough money to cover the costs of growth.

What is better? Higher or lower?

In general, having a lower accounts payable balance is better. This means that you pay your bills on time and are not risking getting into any trouble with your vendors and suppliers.

Of course, as your company grows, your accounts payable will also naturally increase as you purchase more supplies and have more significant bills to pay. Do not worry; this is entirely normal.

If you are growing, you will want to track the accounts payable turnover ratio to ensure the percentage of accounts payable compared to your total purchases remains relatively constant.

Accounts Payable Turnover Ratio =
Total Purchases ÷ Average Accounts Payable

This ratio tells you how frequently you pay your bills. As you grow your business, tracking this number will help you see if your business is paying its bills faster over time or slowing down. Sometimes, vendors will want to know this number to anticipate how quickly you will pay them. You can track this ratio as you grow to make sure that you continue to pay your bills promptly.

How to improve your accounts payable

If your accounts payable is growing, and you need help paying your bills, there are a few strategies you can explore to help reduce your AP, or at least manage it better:

Negotiate with your suppliers.
Most suppliers would rather see you pay their bills than have you default and not pay at all. A simple call to your vendors to negotiate a payment plan can often help ease the pain. This method can also keep you in good standing with your supplier so you can continue to do business with them.

Encourage your customers to pay faster.
For most businesses, getting cash in the door from customers is the best way to help pay bills faster.

160

Establish a business line of credit.
You should do this before you have an accounts payable problem as banks are less likely to lend to you if you already have too much debt. If you do open a credit line, that can help ease the pain of certain times of the month or year where you have less cash on hand than you usually do. Just be careful not to overextend your business and add even more debt.

Instead, think of a credit line as a very temporary loan that allows you to pay your bills while you wait to get paid by your customers.

Lower your costs.
This is probably the most obvious option for lowering your accounts payable, but it is always worth mentioning. When you shop around for different vendors, you might lower your expenses and therefore lower your bills. It is still good to be on the lookout for better deals for your business, so reserve some time every few months to look at your expenses and see where you might be able to cut costs.

Conclusion

Tracking accounts payable is one of the critical components of managing your company cash flow well. You will want to know how much you owe and whom you owe it to.

With the right strategies for managing accounts payable, you will keep a stable cash position crucial for any growing company.

Direct Costs

A quick definition of Direct Costs is "Costs of Goods Sold" (COGS). These are the costs that can be wholly attributed to the production of a specific product or service.

These costs include the direct expenses for materials used to create the product and potentially any labour costs that are exclusively used to develop the product. Direct Costs always excludes indirect expenses, such as marketing expenses, rent, and insurance. Direct costs show up on the Profit and Loss Statement and can be subtracted from revenue to calculate a company's gross margin.

Cost of Goods Sold is a great alternative name for Direct Costs because it refers to costs associated with creating products that a company sells. If you sell services, you probably also have direct costs, but they will be a much smaller percentage of your revenue than they will be for a product company.

For example, a coffee shop would include the costs of coffee and milk in their direct costs. The coffee shop would not include marketing costs, rent, and internet access to calculate direct costs.

Think of direct costs as the exact cost you incur to sell one of your products. You had to either make or buy the product you sold. You may have had to purchase raw materials that you then turned into a product. These costs of producing what you sell are your direct costs.

Deciding what to include in your direct costs varies from one type of business to another. A car company may choose to include manufacturing labour costs for assembling their cars in their direct costs. In contrast, a software development company might consist of labour costs as an indirect cost.

Direct costs are accrued as you sell your product or service, so most companies choose to exclude labour costs from direct costs. This is because your company is incurring the expense of having staff on hand even if you do not sell a single product. Also, that staff might work on multiple products and multiple projects, so it is difficult to determine how much of their salaries should be attributed as a direct cost of producing a specific product.

As a rule of thumb, if you cannot directly associate a specific cost with the sale of a single product, then that cost should NOT be a direct cost. That is why things like rent and marketing expenses are typically not included as direct costs.

While product companies typically have higher direct costs because they deal with physical goods, service companies can have low direct costs. For example, a consulting company may provide a client with 100 hours of consulting, culminating in a final report. If that report is printed and bound, then the direct costs of delivering that consulting are the cost of paper and binding.

The primary expense of providing the consulting project is the labour that went into the project. And, since that labour was probably paid for in salaries, it would not be included in direct costs.

How to calculate and understand your direct costs

Understanding direct costs helps you keep an eye on how much it costs your company to deliver its product or service. If your direct costs are going up, perhaps your suppliers are starting to charge you more, or maybe fuel costs are going up. When your direct costs go up, it might be time to start looking for new suppliers or cut costs in your business.

Direct costs also directly impact your Gross Margin. Gross Margin is your revenue minus your direct costs:

Gross Margin = Revenue – Direct Costs

Because the gross margin is an excellent top-line measure of how efficient your company is at delivering its products and services, keeping an eye on your direct costs helps you understand how efficient your company is.

What is better? Higher or lower direct costs?
Typically, having lower direct costs is better. That means that you deliver your products and services very efficiently and can have a solid gross margin.

Having low direct costs can impact your business in many ways. You could pass on your savings to your customers and offer lower costs than your competition. Or you could look to re-invest in your company and boost your marketing and sales efforts. Or let the savings flow to the bottom line and increase your overall profitability.

Either way, low direct costs positively impact your business, and you should strive to push the number down. Here are a few ideas to improve your direct costs:

Find a new supplier or vendor
It is always useful to comparison shop. Maybe you can get your products and supplies from a new supplier for less.
Perhaps you can shop around and get lower hosting costs for your online service.

Renegotiate with your existing vendors
It is easy to stay with vendors you know, and you can save a lot of business disruption by staying with the same suppliers. So, instead of switching to a new supplier, you can always ask for better pricing. Sometimes the threat of leaving is all you need to get better pricing for your raw materials.

Find efficiencies
If you are a manufacturing company, perhaps you can remove a step from your process, or you can figure out a way to reduce costs in your process. One of the best ways to find efficiencies is to ask the people who work in the manufacturing process. They will know where the waste is and how to lower costs.

Understanding direct costs and how you can lower them is an integral part of running and growing your business. Lowering your direct costs will increase your gross margin and positively impact your profits, so this aspect of your business financials is worth taking the time to understand.

Operating Margins

Let's face it; profit is one of the most important metrics that you track in your business.

Besides tracking your cash, understanding if your company is making money—and keeping it—is the key to long term success and growth.

Because of this, you will need to understand the various components of profitability, why it's essential, and how you can improve it.

While it is tempting to just look at the raw number that is the infamous "bottom line" to determine profitability, it's much more useful to look at profit ratios, otherwise known as "margins".

Margins are earnings displayed as a percentage of total sales or revenue. Using profit-margin percentages lets you easily compare yourself to other businesses to see how you perform compared to your peers. Are you as efficient at generating profits as other businesses like yours? Margins answer this question for you, while absolute profit numbers do not.

For example, let us look at Company X, which had sales of £5 million last year and profits of £300,000. Company Y had sales of £3.5 million and profits of £250,000. Comparing profits, Company X certainly earned more than Company Y. But, if you look at profit margins or the profits generated from each pound of sales, you will see that Company X made six pence for every pound of sales. In comparison, Company Y made more than seven pence. Company X may look bigger, but Company Y is much more efficient and spends less for every pound they make.

Now that you know what margins are and why they are important, let us dig into one of the key profit-margin ratios: Operating Margin, also called Operating Profit Margin.

Operating Margin = Operating Income / Revenue

To calculate the operating margin, you will need to know your operating income. Operating income is your company's earnings before interest and tax expenses, also called EBIT. To calculate your operating income, just subtract your expenses (excluding taxes and interest) from your revenue.

If you have sales of £1 million and an operating income of £100,000, your operating margin would be 10%.

Why is the operating margin important?

Operating margin shows you how good your company is at generating income from normal operations of the business after you have spent money on marketing, sales, product development, etc.

Over time, successful companies should develop a higher operating margin. This means that the company is making more on each pound of sales. To assess whether this is happening, compare the company's quarterly or yearly figures to those of the previous year or quarter and to competitors, if possible.

What is better? Higher or lower?
A higher operating margin is generally better. If operating margins are growing over time, that means that the company is growing sales faster than it is growing expenses. The company is figuring out how to be more efficient and is keeping costs under control.

But start-ups and early-stage companies may have a low operating margin as they invest profits back into the business to continue to fuel growth and expansion. As a business matures, it will usually start to grow its operating margin and generate additional profits.

How to improve your operating margin
To improve your operating margin, you need to either spend less or bring in more revenue. There are a few ways you can go about doing this:

Trim operational "waste"
For example, cut down on raw materials used during the production process.

Make the most of your employees' time
Synchronise production processes, avoid long delays between tasks, and organise time better to avoid bottlenecking. Give idle employees something to do that will cut down on operational waste.

Consolidate processes
Spend some time evaluating and analysing the various systems you use to run your business. If something is inefficient, change it or get rid of it. The goal is to increase efficiency.

Review your expense budget
To understand how to improve your operating margin, you need to know where you are spending money. Look at your payroll expenses, marketing budget, and the cost of materials, and so on. Where is the money going? How can you cut costs?

Compare your figures with industry averages
Once you have figured out where you are spending your income, look at industry averages. How much is the industry spending on each part of its operations? Once you have figured this out, you will be able to look for more specific ways to improve your operating margin.

In simplest terms, operating margin is a measure of your profitability and of your operational efficiency. A higher operating margin means that you are generating more profits for every pound of sales. Unless your focus is to reinvest as much as possible into growing your company, you will want to aim for a higher operating margin.

Net Profit

Net profit is the proverbial bottom line of your business. The money you make does not go back into expenses, taxes, and interest—the net profit that is left over.

In business planning, you will find net profit listed in your financial statements on both the cash flow and as the bottom line of your profit and loss statement. This metric shows you how much your business is bringing in after everything has been paid for. If your business is profitable at the end of the day, this will be a positive (and hopefully large) number.

How to Calculate Net Profit:

So, how do you know where your net profit stands? The standard calculation for net profit (also called net income and/or earnings) is your operating income minus taxes and interest.

Operating income is your revenue from sales minus your operating expenses and cost of goods sold, or "COGS." This means the money comes in from your sales, less all your bills, including sales' direct costs. Operating income is also sometimes referred to as EBITDA, or earnings before interest, taxes, depreciation, and amortization.

Some financial analysts consider operating income to be as important as the net profit itself, so make sure this is a robust sum. You subtract your taxes and any interest payments the company must pay on its loans from this number. The result is your net profit.

The Higher it is, the Better for your Business

Net profit is understandably a metric that you will always want to see positive and as high as it can be. If this number is negative, your business is probably in trouble. You will need to check your cash flow to get an accurate reading of your profit from sales and the actual cash on hand your business must have to stay afloat.

It is essential to remember that a profitable business can still go under if its cash flow is negative.

While your net profit could be a nice high number, if you've got a lot of that money tied up in assets or you're selling heavily on credit, you still need to be sure you have the working capital to cover your bills.

How can you Increase your Net Profit?

Net profit is a question of sales versus expenses. To raise your net profit, consider possible ways to increase your revenue and limit your spending.

Finally, but possibly even more important than ALL the other considerations are Burn Rate. It doesn't matter how much net profit you make from a sale; if it fails to generate sufficient to cover all overall running costs in the time it takes to generate— the income divided by the cost of generating the income— you're going to GROW broke! Or put more simply, you will run out of money whilst generating more money!

Cash Burn Rate

Cash burn rate is the rate at which a company uses up its cash reserves or cash balance. Essentially, it is a measure of the net-negative cash flow.

How fast are you burning through your cash reserves? Or is your cash moving the other direction, building up a healthy balance from positive cash flow?

The cash burn rate is a big concern for funded start-ups. The typical pattern is getting funded, using that cash to build the business, and then aiming to get to positive cash flow before the money runs out. This is sometimes expressed as a *"cash runway"*.

Cash runway is how long your cash will last at your current burn rate.

The same metric is helpful for mature businesses too. How fast are you growing your cash reserve? Or, are you strategically investing that money to fund faster growth? Whatever your plans, be sure to keep an eye on this metric to make sure you are hitting your targets.

How this metric is calculated
To determine the burn rate for a selected period, we find the difference between the starting and ending cash balances for the period.

Did you lose or gain cash?
Then we divide that total by the number of months in the selected period. The result is a monthly value.

For example, say a company started last quarter with £200K in the bank but ended with only £110K. That is a loss of £90K in cash over three months — a burn rate of £30K per month. From a cash runway perspective, that suggests that the company now has just over three months of cash on hand. They need to reduce their burn rate and get cash flow positive soon.

To figure out your 'cash runway' (how long the company has until it runs out of cash), take the rest of the money left in the cash reserves and divide it by the burn rate.

For example, if there is £200,000 left and the burn rate is £50,000 per month, it will take four months for the company to run out of cash.

A lower burn rate is better
It is often best to have a negative burn rate. That means you are building your cash reserves, not using them up. There are cases where investing your cash in growth is a good idea, though: start-ups, obviously, and bootstrapped companies trying to grow. Just make sure you plan for that cash burn and then track your progress. If you burn through your cash reserves faster than expected, you may end up in trouble.

How to reduce your burn rate
If your cash burn rate is higher than you want, the numbers to change are simple. You need to increase your incoming cash, decrease your outgoing cash, or both. Here are ideas on how to do those things:

Increase your revenue
Look for ways to boost your traffic, get more prospects into your pipeline, increase your conversion, or close rates, or raise your pricing. More sales should translate into more cash coming in.

Reduce your payroll expenses
For labour-intensive businesses, deferring new hires, laying off nonessential workers, or limiting benefits can lead to significant savings. Make sure any cuts are SMART and sustainable, in any case.

Reduce your direct costs
For low-margin businesses, finding ways to minimize raw materials and other direct costs can make a big difference in cash flow.

Reduce or defer other expenses
Take a close look at your budget. Are there expenses that are not contributing to your company's success?

Ditch unprofitable revenue streams
It is not uncommon for businesses to offer secondary products or services that don't break even. Why work for free?

Encourage cash sales
Cash sales are great. You get the money right away instead of waiting for it. Make sure you are offering credit terms selectively and smartly, rather than just converting what would have been immediate transactions into delayed ones.

Bill sooner and collect faster
When you offer credit to customers, be sure to bill them promptly, clearly state the credit terms, and follow up with appropriate collection activities if they do not pay on time. Adding late payment charges may also help to bring cash in faster.

Pay your bills slowly
Unless there is a discount or other incentive for paying sooner, do not pay your bills any faster than you have to. Take advantage of the agreed payment terms to hold onto your cash longer.

Sell off excess inventory
Extra inventory is still valuable, but it is not as helpful as having the equivalent amount of cash. Consider offering sales promotions or discounts to sell off what you do not need for regular sales.

Consider using a factoring service
If you cannot get customers to pay their invoices on time, it may be worth looking into such a service.

Hold off on major purchases
If cash is tight, that significant capital expenditure may need to wait — unless it is an investment that will start paying off right away.

Consider refinancing debts
Using too much cash to repay debts? Check with your creditors about options to refinance with lower payments.

Raise additional funds
If you've done all you can to affect your incoming and outgoing cash, but your burn rate is still too high — and, crucially, you are confident that your business can be successful — you may need to do more fundraising. Be sure to do this as early in the process as possible since a business running low on cash may strike potential lenders as too risky.

Credit Control & Cash Collection

The only safe and sustainable method of preventing poor money management within your business is to have a robust Credit Control and Cash Collection process.

Let us assume you are buying in your product from overseas. Until you have an excellent, long term relationship with the supplier (and often not even then), you will need to either pay fully or pay a sizeable deposit for the product before it leaves their country on its way to you.

Straight away, you are in a debit balance for this item and must wait for it to arrive. At which point it maybe you are required to break down the bulk item into individual parts, ready for sale.

Then you begin to sell the item.

Only once the cost of sales has passed the cost of purchase and considers ongoing business operating costs can you begin to see a profit. And, if the company 'runs out' of operating costs before the item breaking a profit, you could be out of business before you begin!

Credit control needs to consider all fixed and operating costs, including both purchasing and sales cost. PLUS, payment terms, to ensure you do not run out of money – the burn rate.

Cash collection effectively manages this process and ensures the business continues to generate (and receive) money faster than the company spends it. Poor cash collection is often another reason for business growth to stagnate and risk failure.

Invoicing a business for the business you have done with them is not cash in the bank. Poor cash collection can result in customers receiving more and more, with less and less intent to settle the bill. I have seen small companies with a 'debtor book' of tens, sometimes hundreds of thousands of pounds. Simply because they are so busy delivering excellent customer service, they failed to acknowledge until they had been paid; it had all been for free!

As you can see, there is much more to consider when understanding money and finances than simply the cost of goods and the cost of sales. However, you would be shocked if you knew of the number of business owners that simply DO NOT understand or have a good grasp of these numbers within their businesses. If I suggested to you that you are going to jump in your car and drive from the UK to Italy, you simply wouldn't do it unless you knew you had the funds to buy the fuel, the car had been recently serviced, all the tyre pressures and brakes had been checked, and that all the lights, signals and fuel gauge worked, right?

Yet, many business owners are 'driving blind' without a good understanding and grasp of the essential numbers present within every business.

An excellent way to overcome this is to set time aside to have money meetings!

Weekly money meetings

Now, it might be essential in a start-up to stop for a few minutes and assess the week's income and expenditure. And yet, as a business continues to grow, so many people stop doing this! There is much to be said for having a constant understanding of the financials within your business, and so a weekly review of the essential numbers within the business should be continued throughout the growth and scale of the company. The more you know, and the more frequently you know it (and the more accurate it is), the more confidence you will have in making the right decisions about the business's continued growth and scale.

Financial dashboard and weekly review

A great way of managing this efficiently would be to set up and operate dashboards within your business.

A financial dashboard (often available within many of the online financial accountancy software) can be an easy and up-to-date method of ensuring you remain updated and informed of your business's economic performance.

However, as with everything else, you will only ever get out what you put in. So before you begin to rely too heavily on the data they, it is imperative that you ensure you are working with the most up to date and accurate data available to you.

Monthly break-even costs

Break-even price is the amount of money, or change in value, for which an asset must be sold to cover the costs of acquiring and owning it. It can also refer to the amount of money for which a product or service must be sold to cover the costs of manufacturing or to provide it. In simple terms, it is the amount of money you need to charge for the sale of your products/services to cover ALL the costs associated with selling them sustainably.

I have seen far too many start-up businesses think that pricing is simply:

- ✓ How much does it cost to buy?
- ✓ How much can I add to that and still sell it?
- ✓ The difference is mine!

I recall one business owner, who had been trading for nearly six years, predominantly selling three services to three different industries. When I asked to view the business numbers, he was very proud to show me his Excel spreadsheet, which we went through in some detail. He almost wept, though, when I was able to demonstrate to him how his most popular service (something he was selling more than 150 times a year) was COSTING him money to provide!

He had failed to consider the total cost of the business operating costs when pricing the service. Once these we re-added to the equation, one service was costing him around £20! It might not be a lot, but it suddenly dawned on him that this oversight in his calculations meant he had been working for the past six years, happily selling this particular service to this industry, which to date had COST him around £7,500!

Break-even analysis is a widely used technique to determine the ongoing business costs and know when it turns profitable. Total variable and fixed costs are compared with the sales revenue to determine the sales volume, sales value, or production at which the company makes neither a profit nor a loss.

It is a powerful tool and should be implemented early into the business and monitored weekly or monthly. Key Performance Indicators (KPIs) for sales teams will eventually be set from it, as will some of the KPI's for marketing teams to ensure sufficient reach for campaigns to enable adequate enquiries for convert.

Management accounts

As a limited company, you are required to submit a set of accounts to Companies House every year. Each time you put them together, you take the valuable opportunity to review them and reflect on the year gone past.

But given it is such a valuable exercise, isn't it something you should be doing more often?

Monthly management accounts are the answer to this much-needed visibility.

Management Accounts allow the business owner to control their business, whereas merely checking the bank balance on a periodic basis does not constitute good financial control.

They will provide the basis for reporting Key Performance Indicators. KPI's are an invaluable tool if reported regularly and in a timely manner.

All businesses must keep certain financial information; however, the statutory information does not help small business owners make informed decisions. Ensuring that the bank balance is always positive and then waiting until the end of the accounting year before knowing the business's financial results is a dangerous strategy.

Easy to use accounting packages offers businesses the opportunity to maintain their books in electronic form, from which Management Accounts can be prepared. Throughout the course of the trading period. The key is to have the data set up in the accounting system so that meaningful Management Accounts can be automatically produced.

What are Management Accounts?

Management Accounts are a set of financial statements prepared periodically, e.g. monthly or quarterly, allowing the business owner or directors to understand the business's financial trading position and make decisions based on the data. These are usually against a plan and typically include a profit and loss account, balance sheet, cash flow statement and a short report.

Suppose the business owner is not competent to prepare the accounts personally. In that case, a bookkeeper will quickly provide such information, particularly if an electronic accounting package is used and configured in the correct format for the business.

Why should a company prepare Management Accounts?
The work may be considered an unwanted administrative chore or simply a cost and another source of cash outflow from the business. However, whilst some administration work is required, the preparation of management accounts is work that should allow informed decisions to be made throughout the year, leading to improved performance. It will also form the basis of the annual results.

What are the benefits of preparing and using Management Accounts?

There are several benefits, including:

Business Control
In some instances, a healthy bank balance may not indicate a successful company. The cash balance is taken at one point in time and may, in the future, be adversely impacted by current

trading conditions. Unless the business owner can immediately identify adverse operating trends and take action to correct the situation, it may result in a severe cash flow shortfall later. Management Accounts should provide sufficient information to detect positive and adverse trends in sales volumes, operating margins, costs, and profit. Importantly this information will be available throughout the trading year and allow for informed business decisions to be taken.

Focus on Key Business Areas

Sales

Knowing at year-end that sales may have increased or decreased in total against the previous period may be interesting, but is it sufficient to exercise control over the business's key areas? As part of the Management Accounts work, it would be expected that an analysis of sales, by product, is made available. This will allow the business owner to review objective data on product sales trends and make informed divestment decisions or investment in different product lines.

Costs

The total business costs are of little value when managing a business. The need to have some cost analysis cannot be underestimated. A business owner/director should know where the company money is being spent and if costs are spiralling out of control.

Tax Planning and Dividend Payments

When up-to-date information is available, a director/owner can plan with greater confidence when transactions need to be made. This approach may help legitimately reduce the company's tax liability and maximise the potential benefits by payment of dividends as opposed to salary.

Demonstrate the Owner is in Control

Knowledge is power. Certainly, suppose the owner can demonstrate that there is a comprehensive understanding of what is happening within the business to the professional people the company has contact with. In that case, respect will be gained, and the business relationship will be heightened. This may be of importance in the relationship with the bank manager.

Reduced Year End Audit and Accounting Costs

During the process of preparing Management Accounts, many queries will be identified and resolved. If this were not the case, at year-end, in addition to accounting for twelve month's work, all queries during the period will need to be addressed at the same time. Memories will fade, and the resolution of issues will take longer and cost more.

Detection of Fraud

A regular review of the business's financial performance will increase the possibility of detecting fraud or other malpractices. The longer time gap between financial reviews will allow wrongdoings to remain hidden and be more challenging to uncover.

The preparation of Management Accounts will provide a valuable tool on which the business owner can manage the business. Informed decisions can be taken based upon objective data and promptly handled to enable the company to succeed.

Money & Margins: Conclusion

I have shared the seven key numbers you must know and manage to maintain a build a profitable business. Manage these closely, frequently and well, and the company shall continue to grow. Take your eye off them, and you quickly risk losing everything. I cannot stress enough how vital these seven numbers are and your continual management of them.

However, once we have established the money (back office) side of the business, it is time to return to the 'front office' and look into sales and understand how to ensure you are always selling WIN|WIN solutions!

Further reading:

If you wanted to learn more about this, I would recommend: No BS Pricing Strategy (Dan Kennedy)

And Profit First by Mike Michalowicz

Chapter Six:

Sales & Negotiation

We established earlier in the book that it is not marketing that gets you business, but awareness. It is what you do with that heightened awareness that brings you the company. That is where sales and negotiation come in.

Sales are the art of converting enquiries into orders for profitable exchange. However, done well, and you can quickly turn one sale into several and a single visit into a raving fan, not only purchasing regularly but also recommending and referring you to others.

Some would argue that a good sales team should not negotiate, so negotiation has no place alongside sales. However, I wholeheartedly disagree. It is just as important to know how to negotiate as it is to sell, to ensure you always under promise and under deliver without leaving any 'spare cash' on the table!

Upselling and cross-selling

Do not ignore your most valuable potential market when expanding your business – your current customers. Upselling and cross-selling is an incredible opportunity for outside sales teams, and neglecting them can be hugely detrimental. Therefore, you should ensure that you have a clearly defined, profitable product upsell/cross-sell strategy.

Competition is as intense as ever in the bid for client trust in sales. Upselling and cross-selling is a way to get ahead of competitors and increase the value of your customers. It is the perfect way to meet your revenue goals in a way that profits your business the most.

Not only can upselling and cross-selling to customers be an excellent opportunity for you, but it also works to help your customers and maintains their trust. Upselling has less to do with pushing more goods and services on a customer and more to do with focusing on meeting your customer's needs.

What is upselling and cross-selling?

Upselling and cross-selling are often used interchangeably in sales conversations, but they are two separate entities. To implement them correctly into your business, you need to understand the differences between them and what they mean for the customer.

Upselling

Upselling is a sales technique where the customer is offered a higher-priced option or add-on to the product/service they are purchasing. Examples of an upsell could be introducing a larger screen to a customer looking at televisions or adding a warranty to the product being sold.

Cross-Selling

On the other hand, cross-selling offers a complimentary product or service that the original product does not cover. For example, offering a credit card to a customer that is opening a checking account. They are related, but not overlapping, products that the customer might find helpful.

The most well-known example to show the distinction between upselling and cross-selling is McDonald's.

Would you like to Supersize that?

This a classic upsell, whilst "Would you like fries with that?" is a cross-sell. One is adding to the product you have, while the other is offering a completely different but complementary product.

Upselling and cross-selling are closely related and useful in both increasing your profit and anticipating your customer's needs. To be successful, though, you must thoroughly understand what your customer is looking for and offer them products at the appropriate time that demonstrate your understanding.

Why Upselling and Cross-Selling is Important

Upselling is essential for businesses, but how exactly? Here are six reasons that both you and your customers want upselling and cross-selling:

Increases Profits

It is no secret that a customer that buys more means that your business will make more money. Growth for your business does not mean simply retaining your customers: it is necessary to continue to grow your wallet allocation for the current customers you have.

The great untapped market in your business might be your existing customers: even amongst customers that strongly trust their bank, only 25% dedicate their total investments to their primary bank. Once you have gained your customer's trust, there is still an incredible number of investments they could be making with you if you use upselling and cross-selling to your advantage.

Increases Customer Loyalty
When businesses refer to upselling, too often, greasy car sales assistants offer services and products that customers don't need to weasel them out of a few pounds. In reality, this could not be further from the truth. The point of upselling is to give the customer all their options to make a knowledgeable choice. It shows customers that you care and expect their needs.

Upselling and cross-selling are closely related to customer satisfaction. They develop loyalty for the banks that they feel look out for their financial well-being. Customer loyalty can be a problem in the sales industry: it is common for customers to lack engagement and leave quickly. Any action that businesses can take to increase loyalty will help minimize the risk of losing customers, especially new customers.

Not only does customer satisfaction mean a reduction in churn rates, but they also offer the best opportunity for free marketing. In the age of information, few people will trust their business to an institution without checking reviews first. Happy customers are the best form of advertisement that you cannot buy.

Increase in ROI
Signing on new customers can be a costly undertaking: for most banks, the average customer may take years until they begin to see a profit. Upselling and cross-selling to your customers allow you to see a profit quickly and receive a better return on your investment. You already did the hard work of marketing, finding, and selling successfully to your customer; your business would be wise to get as much from the interaction as possible.

You leave money on the table when you neglect upselling and cross-selling. Offer customers products relevant to what they are looking to get as much of a return as possible.

Increases Customer Lifetime Value

Not only will upselling or cross-selling bring in a more significant initial profit after signing on the customer, but the overall value of the customer over the course of their lifetime will also be greater.

If you sell a credit card after a home loan for a customer to furnish their new house, for example, you will be bringing in much more profit over the course of the years than you would with a mortgage payment alone.

Not only will you increase their lifetime value by increasing the amount they buy, but by increasing their loyalty. You will see much more from a customer that stays loyal to you. Again, the increase in customer loyalty will pay off over the long run.

Balances Growth between New and Existing Customers

Research has shown that increasing customer retention by as little as 5% increases profits anywhere from 25% up to 95%. Maintaining a balance between the customers you sign on initially and the ones you maintain is essential to your institution's survival.

Maintain a healthy ratio of new to existing customers to ensure that your business is making a profit. While gaining new clientele is a healthy goal, also keep in mind ways to keep the clients that you sign on. One way to do this is through upselling and cross-selling. Customers who feel that their bank continues to look after their needs by offering relevant and helpful products and services will be far more likely to stay.

Offers Convenience and Flexibility for Customers
The benefits of upselling and cross-selling are not just for businesses. It works so well for businesses because it works well for customers too.

Many customers do not want to shop around for a new institution when they need a particular product or service. By offering them more choices or relevant add-ons, they do not have to risk a new company to get what they need.

Most customers will stay with what they like if they know what is available. Since you have established trust with the customer, you can have the first shot of their business by telling them the related products and services you offer. When you upsell or cross-sell to a customer, you give them the convenience of staying with you and the flexibility to choose what they need.

Strategies for Successful Upselling and Cross-Selling

Now that you know the importance of upselling, you need to establish a successful upselling strategy to grow your business. Upselling is a delicate matter, but you will find a great untapped market if proper care is taken. Here are some methods to upselling:

Trust is Vital

Customer relationships are all about trust. You build this trust by getting to know their wants and needs. When you understand your customer, you can easily anticipate their needs and offer them suitable products and services. How do you come to understand them?

Communication

It is vital to keep engaged and in contact with customers and potential customers to know what they want. Customer's trust will then earn a more expanded business.

#ADDAZERO – Building the Foundation on which to SCALE

Track the Customer Journey

To make sure you are upselling the right products to the correct customer at the proper time, it is essential to flag potential upsells by tracking the customer journey.

Customers tend to communicate through more than one medium when they are serious about purchasing, so keep track of them through a CRM.

An integrated CRM will let your entire company understand the specific customer and allow anyone to cross-sell and add to the customer journey.

Customer journey data can predict the likelihood of responding to an upsell offer. Customers have come to expect personalized and relevant information.

To successfully upsell, you need to make an offer pertinent to that specific customer based on preferences and recent interactions.

Be a Sales Consultant versus a Salesman

Become an expert in what your customer needs. This way, instead of merely trying to "sell" a product to a potential client, you can suggest ways that your other products can serve your customer. Understand your customer's business and how it relates to your product.

Find places that they could improve by using your product or service. You are in the perfect place to make suggestions because you are a product expert and have insights to offer that they cannot find elsewhere. This expert understanding can make you come across as a sales consultant versus just a salesman.

Be Relevant to the Customer

Although upselling and cross-selling can be great tools for the customers, few things annoy the customer more than wading through products and services that do not relate to them or their experiences. Relevance is key in upselling and cross-selling.

188

Is your customer buying a house, starting a business, starting their first job? These are essential factors to keep in mind when considering what products or services will or will not work for them specifically. Do not try to sell an auto loan to someone coming to you about a business loan.

It comes down to knowing your customer. Keeping track of your customer and their needs will help ensure that you are making relevant recommendations to enhance your relationship.

Tapping into Your Best Market
If your business is not utilizing upselling and cross-selling, you are leaving money at the table. Offer your customers relevant products to make sure that they are getting your full range of services and you are getting the best ROI possible.

Good negotiations are crucial as they contribute much to business success and build better relations. Any negotiation aims to reach an agreement that results in mutual benefits. Good negotiation means leaving each party satisfied and willing to do business with each other in the future. By doing so, turning a one-off purchase into the start of a buyer/seller relationship.

Most of us negotiate because we want to do a beneficial deal for all the parties involved. However, negotiation is not about compromise nor setting up barriers that need defending.

Let us assume the prospect has come into the store intending to redecorate a room in their new home. They have a long list of items they require, and whilst you do sell all the items required, some are currently out of stock.

The customer has taken the time and effort to visit your store and not simply order the items from Amazon, and so how you negotiate with them, by offering to place a 'special order' straight away for the 'missing' items. Either have them delivered directly to the customer's new home or available for collection before the weekend will determine if you make a sale or not.

Negotiation is not about discount or compromise; it ensures we always deliver WIN | WIN solutions.

Conversion rate

It might sound like some sort of religious metric, but it is one of the best ways to measure your advertising campaigns' performance.

What is Conversion Rate?

Unlike click-through rate or cost-per-click, conversion rate describes how good your marketing is at getting people to do what you want them to do (often referred to as converting). The higher your conversion rate, the better your marketing is!

To put it simply, your conversion rate is the percentage of visitors to your website or landing page that convert (do what you want them to do). Depending on your business goals, a *"conversion"* could be almost anything, but here are a few common types of conversions:

- ✓ Making a purchase
- ✓ Submitting a form (contact us form, lead gen form, etc.)
- ✓ Calling your business
- ✓ Engaging with your online chat
- ✓ Signing up for a subscription (either paid or free—like a newsletter)
- ✓ Registering on the site
- ✓ Downloading something (software trial, eBook, mobile app, etc.)
- ✓ Using something (new/advanced feature on your software or app, simply using your software/app for a certain amount of time)
- ✓ Upgrading their service
- ✓ Engaging with your site in some way (time on site, repeat visits, number of pages visited)

ADDAZERO – Building the Foundation on which to SCALE

There are plenty of other conversion actions people can take on a site, but this should give you a feel for a "conversion". A conversion is a measurable action that progresses a potential customer towards becoming a paying customer.

How Do I Calculate Conversion Rate?

Calculating conversion is relatively easy. All you must do is divide the number of conversions you get in each time frame, by the total number of people who visited your site or landing page and multiply it by 100%.

Conversion rate = (conversions / total visitors) x 100%

For example, if your site had 17,492 visitors and 2,305 conversions last month, your conversion rate is 13.18%. Easy enough, right? If you set you're tracking up right, most online advertising (e.g. AdWords, Facebook Ads) and analytics platforms (e.g., Google Analytics) can show you your conversion rate.

One of the great things about conversion rate is that you can be as specific or as broad as you want to be. Here are a few different types of conversion rate you can use and ways you can use this data to examine performance:

✓ **Overall conversion rate** - How well does your website convert traffic from any source?
✓ **Marketing channel conversion rate** - Is AdWords traffic or Facebook Ads traffic more likely to convert?)
✓ **Page-level conversion rate** - Which of these pages is better at converting traffic?)
✓ **Campaign conversion rate** - Did my targeting changes improve anything?)
✓ **Individual ad conversion rate** - Do I need to change my ad copy? Does this ad drive more qualified traffic?)
✓ **Keyword conversion rate** - Which keywords deserve more budget?)

This list just scratches the surface. Conversion rate is an excellent metric for evaluating the performance of almost any aspect of your online marketing. Driving clicks is great, but if those clicks do not do something beneficial for your business, something needs to change.

Conversion Rate vs Click Conversion Rate

Now, you might be thinking, *"But what if the same person converts multiple times? How does that affect my conversion rate? Should I count that as one conversion or multiple conversions?"*

Those are all great questions. To deal with the whole *"total conversions vs converting visitors"* problem, marketers use different terms to describe each situation.

As we discussed above, the conversion rate is the number of conversions divided by the number of visitors. To see what percentage of visitors converted (regardless of how many times they converted), you divide converting visitors by total visitors and multiply by 100%. We typically call this your *"click conversion rate"*.

**Click conversion rate =
(converting visitors / total visitors) x 100%**

Again, with the right conversion tracking in place, most online advertising and analytics platforms allow you to view your click conversion rate.

Their conversion rate is virtually identical to their click conversion rate for many businesses, so we shall focus on conversion rate here. However, the click conversion rate can be handy when you get many repeat conversions and want to see what percentage of your actual visitors are converting.

Getting Meaningful Data

One thing to keep in mind as you calculate your conversion rate is the quality of your data. For example, I have seen campaigns and pages with a 100% conversion rate, which seems great until you realise that they only had one visitor.

If your traffic sample is not very big, it's hard to trust your results. If 5% of 20 people convert on your site and one of them converted by accident (it happens), is your page working very well? Probably not since your only conversion was an accident.

On the other hand, if 5% of 10,000 people convert and 5 of them converted by accident, your conversion rate drops from 5% to 4.95%. That is still reliable data.

Every traffic source has a certain amount of natural randomness (accidental conversions, people who meant to convert but didn't, random periods of high or low conversion rates etc.). The only effective way to look at your conversion rates is to use a sufficiently long timeframe.

Of course, like most other conversion rate-related concepts, there is no "right" timeframe for every business. Many marketers like to use a month as their go-to timeframe, but if you are a big site like Tesco, you might only need a day to get meaningful data. If you only get a few hundred visits a month, it may take six months to really get a feel for your conversion rate.

What is a Good Conversion Rate?

As you can probably imagine, conversion rates vary considerably depending on your traffic quality, industry, business, what you are selling and even the specific conversion action you are tracking.

Also, it is essential to remember that a conversion is not always the same thing as a purchase. While the conversion rate is a handy metric, most marketing aims not to produce conversions—it's to generate sales.

Conversion Rate Tracking

While conversion rate may not be the ultimate measure of success, it is an excellent tracking performance tool. But, to calculate your conversion rate, you need to be tracking conversions. As I mentioned earlier, with a bit of extra effort, you can track conversions directly through most advertising and analytics platforms.

With all the possible conversions and platforms out there, covering how to implement conversion tracking is a chapter in and of itself, but here is a quick reference list for several big-name platforms:

- ✓ Google AdWords
- ✓ Google Analytics
- ✓ Facebook Ads (includes Instagram Ads)
- ✓ Twitter Ads
- ✓ Pinterest Promoted Pins

Setting up conversion tracking is easiest if you have a good developer around, but trust me, good conversion tracking is worth the effort. You cannot improve what you don't understand, and if you are not tracking the results of your online marketing, how do you know what is working and what isn't?

The good news is that tracking and using your conversion rate puts you in a relatively elite group of online marketers, giving you a significant competitive advantage.

Conversion Rate Optimisation

Knowing what a conversion rate is and how to track it is one thing, but what do you do with your conversion rate data? More importantly, how do you improve your conversion rate?

Conversion rate optimisation (CRO) is the process of optimising your landing page and website to—you guessed it—produce more conversions from your traffic!

The great thing about CRO is that it helps you get the most out of the traffic you already have. For example, even without increasing traffic to your site, improving your conversion rate from 1% to 2% will double your conversions.

Can you see why CRO is such an important part of your online marketing strategy? If you are not optimising your conversion rate, you are wasting money.

Testing Your Website

So, how do you get at all those lost conversions? It is not as difficult as you might think. Here are a few ways to start doing CRO today:

Create a Dedicated Landing Page
If you are doing any sort of paid advertising (AdWords, Bing Ads etc.), you should be sending your traffic to a dedicated landing page. There are so many good reasons to do this, but the biggest reason is page optimisation. If you are going to pay to get traffic to your site, you want to send them to a page that is designed to sell.

Landing pages are also the most accessible type of page to do CRO on. If you are still sending your traffic to your homepage, this is the first place I would start.

Come Up with a Hypothesis
All good CRO tests start with a hypothesis. But, to put your hypothesis together, you will have to make some educated guesses about which site elements have the most significant impact on your conversion rate and profitability.

Here are a few areas you can look at first:

Headline
Your headline needs to sell and sell hard. 80% of your audience will not get past your headline, so you should at least test your headline even if you don't test anything else.

Offer
Your audience is not you, so they do not always respond the way you think they will.

Try different descriptions and layouts to see what resonates best with your prospective clients.

Call-to-action
Like your offer, the right call-to-action (CTA) may take a few tests to discover. Try more descriptive CTAs or different button sizes.

Media
Sometimes a new picture or video can make all the difference.

Once you have a hypothesis and two-page designs to assess, all you must do is get your test running!

A/B Test
The easiest way to start doing CRO is the A/B test. If you have got traffic coming out of your ears, you can do some cool (and complicated) multivariate testing, but for most companies, A/B testing is the easiest and most effective way to go.

To run an A/B test, all you do is set up two different variants of a page and split your traffic between them. Half of your traffic goes to variant A, and half goes to variant B.

To split your traffic, you will need the help of some sort of CRO software. If you are serious about CRO, there are some fantastic, albeit expensive ways to run your A/B test. But, if you are just starting out, here are some cheaper options to try first:

Google Content Experiments

This is free, so you do not have any excuse for not testing; however, it does not give you real-time results, so it may not be an excellent option for everyone.

Unbounce
If you only need to A/B test a landing page, Unbounce is the way to go. It is a powerful and easy-to-use system that allows you to create and test various landing pages quickly.

Optimizely
This is a more expensive option than Google experiments, but it also has some extra features that provide additional CRO insight.

Visual Website Optimizer
VWO is slightly cheaper than Optimizely and has a very intuitive interface, so it's one of our favourite CRO platforms at Disruptive Advertising.

Each of these testing platforms will allow you to test different versions of your website or landing page and see which version has the best conversion rate.

Testing Your Traffic

In addition to testing your website, another great way to improve your conversion rate is to test your traffic. Obviously, if most of your traffic comes from organic search results on Google, that's not an option, but if you happen to be running any sort of pay-per-click campaign, you have a lot more control over who is visiting your site or landing page and why.

This is important because the wrong traffic will not convert, even on the perfect page.

So, how do you make sure you are sending the right traffic to your landing page? Here are four things to consider.

Do Your Homework

Before you even start working on ad copy or a landing page, you should first take the time to do a little research on your target audience.

Consider things such as:

- ✓ Have you advertised to this segment before? What worked? What did not?
- ✓ If this is a new audience for you, talk to some people in your target audience. Run a couple of ideas past them. Often, what works for you does not work for your audience.
- ✓ What is the best way to target your audience? Are there specific intent-based keywords they use? Particular interests in social media? Do they have a certain income level, fashion preference or another defining trait you can use to target them?

Once you have nailed down these details, use them to build your targeting strategy. A little bit of forethought can help you avoid wasting a lot of money.

Create the Scent

The content of your marketing material should match the content of your landing page.

However, the reverse is also true. If you want to market a product or offer to a specific audience, your ads need to connect your target audience's needs and interests to what they will find on your landing page.

In effect, you need to *"create the scent."*

Ideally, your message should be so well crafted that only people who would be interested in the content of your landing page will click on your ad and—when they hit your landing page—they should immediately feel like they're in the right place.

Get Granular

Expanding on the previous point, it is perfectly okay to have different marketing material and different landing pages for each type and subtype of the audience. Remember, each audience has various reasons for coming to your landing page and will respond to your page in unique ways. So, the more audience-specific you can make your ads and landing page, the more likely they are to convert.

Depending on your advertising medium, there are various ways to do this: single-keyword ad groups (SKAGs) for PPC, social media targeting options, YouTube interests etc. Just remember, the more granular your ads and landing pages, the better your conversion rate will be.

Pay for What Works

Finally, as you identify traffic sources with consistently poor (especially unprofitable) conversion rates, either change something or quit spending money on that traffic source. You do not have to keep investing in the wrong traffic!

Instead, create a testing budget for exploring new traffic or targeting opportunities and focus most of your budget on known winners.

And, since you are now pointing the right sort of traffic at your landing pages, you can expect your A/B tests to really start producing. You have got the right audience on your page; make sure the user experience is irresistible!

Conclusion

Conversion rate is one of the most important marketing metrics. Unlike click-through rate, conversion rate tells you what percentage of your traffic is doing what you want them to do. You can buy all the clicks you want, but if those clicks don't convert... something is wrong.

Now that you know what conversion rate is, how to use it and how to improve your conversion rates, it is time to put conversion rate data to work for you!

Sales System

A sales system gets salespeople organised, helps them manage contacts better, makes tracking sales deals more efficient and saves them time. In short, a sales system is a tool that makes managing your sales opportunities effortless.

Whether you're a salesperson, a sales manager or a business owner, sales management software can help you sell more by keeping you focused on the right deals and making sure you never forget to follow up with a prospect.

Essential features of a Sales System

The list of items you should look for in your sales system is long, and due diligence is essential in making your choice. The most important aspect is choosing a tool that suits your specific needs best; this often means customising it.

Benefits of a Sales System

- ✓ Reduces admin work: Manual data entry is a thing of the past, or at least it should be. With the right tool, you will have to do less data handling and have more time to sell.
- ✓ Easy to use and set up: Instead of being a weekly reporting platform, sales management software should be an easy one-stop shop for all your sales tracking needs.
- ✓ Unifies all tools: Having a single, streamlined view of your sales process clarifies and gets your team on the same page. Supporting apps and integrations is also a must.
- ✓ Fully customisable: Flexible sales systems that are easy to adjust yourself are the best way to mould the perfect

software for your business. The less complicated it is to change, the easier it is to personalise.

✓ Available on the go: Mobile access is crucial when you are actively selling. CRM apps make sales management on the move easy and simple, and it is even more challenging for information to fall through the cracks.

✓ Designed for salespeople: Salespeople need software designed for their trade. While using regular CRMs can work, the real magic happens when you use tools that were built to drive sales and manage leads.

Sales Scripts

Many salespeople believe they will not sound good if they read from a sales script.

While I agree you should never read from a script when selling, a sales script can significantly improve your results by preparing you with the best questions and lines to say and ask.

How to Write a Sales Script

First, let us walk through the sales script creation process. You can follow this framework to craft your pitching strategy—then simply plug in your unique value props into the template.

Identify a product or service to focus on

Start by identifying the product or service you would like to ultimately sell to the prospect.

Home in on your target audience

You can certainly create one sales script that works for every type of prospect—but it is more effective to adapt your questions and points to the specific buyer persona. In this step, consider the different types of buyers you will be selling to.

Develop your benefits

Take the product you selected and then think about the buyer that you are planning on talking to. How does the product help them increase productivity, cut costs, improve accuracy, etc.? Come up with at least three benefits.

Link your benefits to pain points
Build a list of pain points to discuss by looking at the benefits you identified in the previous step. There is usually a related pain point that is resolved, minimised, or avoided for each benefit.

Ask questions about those pain points
The best salesperson is the one who asks the best questions. To develop a robust list of questions, look at each pain point identified in step number four. Use one or two questions per pain point to determine if it's a relevant challenge for the prospect.

Don't talk too much
If you are doing more talking than listening, you are doing it wrong. A script should leave ample time for your prospect to ask questions, share comments, and generally be heard.

Record yourself giving your pitch to a friend or colleague. When you go back and listen, if more than half the pitch is you talking, rethink your approach, edit your script, and include more moments to ask your prospect questions.

Example questions for your sales script:

- ✓ *"So, what I hear from you is [repeat what you've heard from your prospect]. Is that right?"*
- ✓ *"What are your goals this quarter?"*
- ✓ *"Is this relevant to your company goals this year?"*
- ✓ *"What's your single biggest pain point right now?"*
- ✓ *"How long have you been thinking about this?"*
- ✓ *"Is there anything I've overlooked?"*
- ✓ *"What's your biggest priority at the moment?"*
- ✓ *"How will this solution make your life easier?"*

✓ *"What is your manager hoping to accomplish in the next year?"*
✓ *"Have I earned two more minutes of your time?"*

Work a few of these questions into your script and entice your prospect to answer. It is an easy way to keep the conversation going and learn more about them.

Always close for something
It might be as simple as asking for five minutes more of your prospect's time. Or it might be asking for their business.

Your talk track should always be about your prospect. Do not finish with 'Does that make sense?' or 'Is this something you'd be interested in?' These closing questions feel like a quiz and are more about you than them.

Instead, close with, 'We have clients who love being able to build software anywhere in the world. How many software engineers do you have at your company?'"

This question does not assume your prospect followed your whole pitch. If you lost them, this type of question will gain their attention back.

But every time you send your prospect a message, make sure you have a call to action for them.

Unique Selling Proposition (USP)

Before you can begin to sell your product or service to anyone else, you must sell yourself on it. This is especially important when your product or service is like those around you. Very few businesses are one-of-a-kind. Just look around you: How many clothing retailers, hardware stores, air conditioning installers and electricians are truly unique?

The key to effective selling in this situation is what advertising and marketing professionals call a "unique selling proposition"

(USP). Unless you can pinpoint what makes your business unique in a world of homogeneous competitors, you cannot successfully target your sales efforts.

Pinpointing your USP requires some hard soul-searching and creativity. One way to start is to analyse how other companies use their USPs to their advantage. This requires careful analysis of other companies' ads and marketing messages. If you analyse what they say they sell, not just their product or service characteristics, you can learn a great deal about how companies distinguish themselves from competitors.

Here is how to uncover your USP and use it to power up your sales:

Put yourself in your customer's shoes.

Too often, entrepreneurs fall in love with their product or service and forget that it is the customer's needs, not their own, that they must satisfy. Step back from your daily operations and scrutinise what your customers *really* want. Suppose you own a pizza parlour. Sure, customers come into your pizza place for food. But is food all they want? What could make them come back repeatedly and ignore your competition? The answer might be quality, convenience, reliability, friendliness, cleanliness, courtesy, or customer service.

Remember, price is never the only reason people buy. Suppose your competition is beating you on pricing because they are more prominent. In that case, you must find another sales feature that addresses the customer's needs and then build your sales and promotional efforts around that feature.

Know what motivates your customers' behaviour and buying decisions.

Effective marketing requires you to be an amateur psychologist. You need to know what drives and motivates customers. Go beyond the traditional customer demographics, such as age, gender, race, income, and geographic location, that most businesses collect to analyse their sales trends. For our pizza shop example, it is not enough to know that 75 per cent of your customers are in the 18-to-25 age range. You need to look at their motives for buying pizza—taste, peer pressure, convenience and so on.

Uncover the real reasons customers buy your product instead of a competitor's. As your business grows, you will be able to ask your best source of information – your customers. For example, the pizza entrepreneur could ask them why they like his pizza over others, plus ask them to rate the importance of the features he offers, such as taste, size, ingredients, atmosphere, and service. You will be surprised at how honest people are when you ask how you can improve your service.

If your business is just starting out, you will not have a lot of customers to ask yet, so "shop" your competition instead. Many retailers routinely drop into their competitors' stores to see what and how they are selling. If you are brave, try asking a few of the customers after leaving the premises they like and dislike about the competitors' products and services.

Once you have gone through this three-step market intelligence process, you need to take the next--and hardest--step: clearing your mind of any preconceived ideas about your product or service and being brutally honest. What features of your business jump out at you as something that sets you apart? What can you promote that will make customers want to patronize your business? How can you position your business to highlight your USP?

Do not get discouraged. Successful business ownership is not about having a unique product or service; it is about making your product stand out even in a market filled with similar items.

Sales & Negotiation: Conclusion

Sales is an art. Done well, it builds lasting relationships with people who see the value you provide to them and their lives. Poorly done, and it is most off-putting and damaging to both you and your brand. It can be learnt but requires time and consideration. Overall, it is understanding that the best in the business sell without selling by crossing the boundaries between sales and customer service.

Further reading:

There are a few fabulous books if you would like to learn much more about this:

Influence*: The psychology of persuasion (Robert B. Cialdini)*

The little red book of selling *(Jeffrey Gitomer)*

*Or pretty much **anything** by (David Sandler) www.Sandler.com*

.

Chapter Seven:

Service & Delivery

You can have the very best product/service globally, yet you are nothing but a dream without customers. And yet, SO many business owners fail to give enough consideration to their customers!

Sure, they claim to provide *"great customer service"* but, as you will find within this chapter, that is nothing new, nothing unique and nothing to write home about.

This chapter will uncover subtle, but exponential difference between reactive and proactive, and how even considering it, a customer SERVICE department is already on a downward spiral!

Customer journey

A customer journey map is a visual representation of every experience your customers have with you. It helps to tell the story of a customer's experience with your brand from original engagement and into, hopefully, a long-term relationship.

At first glance, a customer's journey is quite simple. You offer something; they buy it. But once you get into the detail, customer journeys are quite complex and come in many varieties. Your customers can encounter your business in a multitude of ways and from many different starting points, for example, marketing, referrals, search, social media, customer service enquiries and above-the-line campaigns.

No doubt you want to make every experience a customer has as good as it can be. So, to make sure no interaction slips through the cracks, you need to map out every touchpoint or experience along the customer journey.

What is customer journey mapping?

Customer journey mapping helps businesses step into their customer's shoes and see their business from the customer's perspective. It helps companies gain insights into common customer pain points, improve the customer experience, and define what customers and prospective customers need to complete a purchase.

From a customer's perspective, they want their experience with a brand to be connected and seamless. They expect companies to know and remember, across multiple touchpoints, who they are and what they are looking for so that the necessary information is available and without the necessity to repeat or clarify their needs. A map helps reveal issues with siloes in your business.

The benefits of a customer journey map include:

- ✓ helping you see where customers interact with your business
- ✓ focusing the business on customer needs at different stages in the buying funnel
- ✓ identifying whether the customer journey is in a logical order
- ✓ giving an outside perspective on your sales process
- ✓ showing the gaps between the desired customer experience and the one received
- ✓ highlighting development priorities allowing you to concentrate efforts and expenditure on what matters most to maximise effectiveness

Getting the most from customer journey mapping

To make your map as useful as possible, you need to include every point where your customer encounters your business, from packaging and manuals to TV ads and Facebook posts. Maps can contain quantitative elements from things like your website analytics, CRM, or call centre software. For instance, a map might highlight that your call centre provides swift answers and satisfying service by overlaying data, but your live chat is causing frustration.

As your relationship with a customer develops, your map will also cover the long-term, post-purchase journey they take with you. Looking at many customers' completed journeys can help highlight a clear route from research and inquiry to sale, mapping potential obstacles and opportunities for the business to improve the trip.

Benchmarking against your brand promise

A customer journey map also reveals how well the customer experience matches up to your brand promise. For example, you might portray your customer experience as effortless. But when a customer arrives at a store to collect items they have bought online, only to face long queues and confusion about their order, their experience does not match up. This kind of scenario will play out in various ways depending on your product, service, or business type. You need to understand where these mismatches are happening and start to fix the issues – and the map helps you do this.

By optimising and improving the experiences along the journey, you will be building solid, long-term relationships with your customers.

Safeguarding your future

Many consumers are shifting from offline to online, using various digital tools to help them with their purchasing decisions. Offline interactions are also taking on a digital dimension, with location-based services adding to the experience of visiting a store or taking a flight. And as more 'digital natives' enter the world of work and gain purchasing power, online interactions grow commercial importance. Your customer is likely to use search, online review sites and social networks as the first port of call when evaluating a possible purchase.

Understanding how these interactions work and how to take advantage of them is vital to business success.

A customer journey map is just the first step to staying on top of this change. Businesses need increasingly sophisticated processes and tools, and that requirement is likely to increase in future – the number of touchpoints is increasing by around 20% a year, according to McKinsey. With more touchpoints comes more complexity in servicing customer needs successfully. A map should help highlight areas where technology can ease the burden and challenges faced by your business.

How to map your customer journey

Today's consumer interacts with brands in ways that are tricky to pin down – from gaining awareness of a brand via social media to receive a *"thank you for your purchase"* email after a successful transaction. There are usually many and various steps in between.

This is not something you can assume or predict based on your internal perspective. A customer journey is particular to the physical experiences your customers have. Thus, the best way to understand the customer journeys of your customers is by asking them.

However, merely understanding the customer journey is not enough. It is best to visualise it into a diagram that you and other employees can refer to as a resource. This is where a customer journey map comes into play.

A customer journey map is a visual representation of a customer or prospect's process to achieve a goal with your company. With the help of a customer journey map, you can get a sense of your customers' motivations – their needs and pain points.

By understanding what these motivations are, you can understand how to structure your touchpoints to create the most effective and efficient process for your customers. A customer journey map maps out the current process, from the first to the final touchpoint, to see if your customers are currently reaching the goals and, if not, how they can.

Because the customer journey can no longer be represented in a linear journey from A to B – buyers often take a back and forth, cyclical, multi-channel journey – the mapping can be hard to visualise.

For this reason, savvy business leaders use various ways of representing the journey, from post-it notes on a boardroom wall to Excel spreadsheets to infographics. The most important thing is that the map makes sense to those who will be using it.

However, before you can dive into creating your customer journey map, you need first to collect data from customers and prospects. The process of creating an effective customer journey map is extensive but valuable.

Why it is important.

You can refocus your company with an inbound perspective.

Rather than trying to discover your customers through outbound marketing, you can have your customers find you with the help of inbound marketing. Outbound marketing involves poorly targeted tactics at generalised or uninterested audiences and seeking to interrupt customers from their daily lives.

Outbound marketing is costly and inefficient. It annoys and deters customers and prospects. Inbound marketing is creating exciting content that is useful and that your customers are already searching for. It grabs their attention first and focuses on the sales later.

By mapping out the customer journey, you can understand what is exciting and helpful to your customers about your company and website and turn them away. You can create the kind of content that will attract them to your company and keep them there.

You can create a new target customer base.

If you do not adequately understand the customer journey, you probably don't fully know your customers' demographics and psychographics. This is dangerous; it is a waste of time and money to repeatedly target too broad an audience rather than who will be interested in your products, services, and content.

Researching your typical customers' needs and pain points and mapping out their journey will give you a good picture of the kinds of people who are trying to achieve a goal with your company. Thus, you can hone in your marketing to that specific audience.

You can create a customer-focused mentality throughout the company.

As your company gets larger, it can be hard to coordinate all the departments to be as customer-focused as your customer service, support, and success teams. They can often have sales and marketing goals that are not based on what real customers want.

A clear customer journey map can be shared with your entire organisation. The great thing about these maps is that they map out every step of the customer journey from initial attraction to post-purchase support. And, yes, this concerns marketing, sales, and service.

How to Create a Customer Journey Map

Based on this rationale, you cannot deny the importance of a customer journey map. Thus, we have created the following steps for crafting the best map to help your company and customers prosper.

Follow these steps, and you cannot go wrong:

Set clear objectives for the map

Before you can dive into creating your map, you need to ask yourself why you are making one in the first place. What are your goals? Who is it specifically about? What experience is it based upon?

Based on this, you may want to create a buyer persona. This is a fictitious customer with all their demographics and psychographics, who represents your customer avatar. Having a clear persona helps remind you to direct every aspect of your customer journey map towards them.

Profile your personas and define their goals

Next, you should conduct research. Some great ways to get valuable customer feedback is through questionnaires.
The important thing is to only reach out to actual customers or prospects. You want the input of people interested in purchasing your products and services. Who have interacted with your company before or plan to do so.

Some examples of good questions to ask are:

- ✓ How did you hear about our company?
- ✓ What first attracted you to our website?
- ✓ What are the goals you want to achieve with our company? In other words, what problems are you trying to solve?
- ✓ How long have you/do you typically spend on our website?
- ✓ Have you ever purchased with us? If so, what was your deciding factor?
- ✓ Have you ever interacted with our website with the intent of making a purchase but decided not to? If so, what led you to this decision?
- ✓ On a scale of 1 to 10, how easy is it for you to navigate our website?
- ✓ Did you ever require customer support? If so, how helpful was it on a scale of 1 to 10?
- ✓ Is there any way that we can further support you to make your process easier?

You can use this buyer persona tool to fill in the details you procure from customer feedback.

List out all the touchpoints

Touchpoints are all the places on your website where you interact with your customers. Based on your research, you should list out all the touchpoints your customers and prospects are currently using, as well as the ones you believe they should be using if there is no overlap.

This is an important step in creating a customer journey map because it gives you insight into your customers' actions.

If they use fewer touchpoints than expected, does this mean they are quickly getting turned away and leaving your site early? If they are using more than expected, does this mean your website is complicated and requires several steps to reach an end goal?

Whatever the case may be, understanding the touchpoints can help you understand customer journeys' ease and objectives.

This does not just mean your website. You need to look at all how your customer might come across you online.

These might include:

- ✓ Social channels
- ✓ Paid ads
- ✓ Email marketing
- ✓ Third-party review sites or mentions.

Run a quick Google search of your brand to see all the pages that mention you. Verify these by checking in on your Google Analytics to see where your traffic is coming from.

Whittle your list down to those touchpoints that are the most common and will most likely see an action associated with it.

Actions

List out all the actions your customers perform throughout their interaction with your brand. This might be a Google search for your keywords or clicking on an email from you. You may wind up with a long list of actions. That is fine. You will get a chance to rationalise your information later.

It is important to recognise when customers are being expected to take too many actions to achieve their goals. Reducing the number of steps a customer needs to take can feel risky but pays off in higher conversion rates.

Emotions & Motivations
All marketing is a result of cause and effect. Likewise, every action your customer takes is motivated by emotion. And your customer's feelings will change depending on which part of their journey they are at.

A pain point or a problem usually causes the emotional driver of each of your customer's actions. Knowing this will help you provide the right content at the right time to smooth the customer's emotional journey through your brand.

Obstacles & Pain Points
Get to know what roadblocks are stopping your customer from taking their desired action. One common obstacle is cost. For example, one of your customers could love your product but abandon their cart on discovering unexpectedly high shipping rates.

Highlighting these potential obstacles in your customer journey can help you to mitigate them. For example, you could provide an FAQ page that answers common questions about shipping costs.

Identify the elements you want your map to show.

Types of Customer Journey Maps

There are four types of customer journey maps that each have their benefits. Depending on the specific purpose you have for the map, you can choose the one that is right for you.

Current State
These customer journey maps are the most widely used type. They visualise the actions, thoughts, and emotions your

216

customers currently experience while interacting with your company. They are best used for continually improving the customer journey.

Day in the Life
These customer journey maps visualise the actions, thoughts, and emotions your customers currently experience in all activities
in which they partake daily, whether that includes your company. This type gives a broader lens into your customers' lives and their pain points in real life. They are best used for addressing unmet customer needs before customers know they even exist.

Future State
These customer journey maps visualise what you believe will be the actions, thoughts, and emotions your customers experience in future interactions with your company. Based on what the current experience is, you map out where you want to be. They are best used for illustrating your vision and setting a clear objective.

Service Blueprint
These customer journey maps begin with a simplified version of one of the above map styles. Then, they layer on the factors responsible for delivering that experience, including people, policies, technologies, and processes. They are best used to identify the root causes of current customer journeys or identify the steps needed to attain desired future customer journeys.

Take the customer journey yourself.

Just because you have designed your map, it does not mean your work is done. The next stage is the essential part of the process: analysing the results.

How many people are clicking on your website but then closing out before making a purchase? How can you better support customers? These are some of the questions you should be able to answer with your finished map.

Analysing the results can show you where customer needs are being unmet. By approaching this, you can ensure that you provide a valuable experience and make it clear that people can find solutions to their problems with your company's help.

The whole exercise of mapping the customer journey remains hypothetical until you try it out yourself.

For each persona, follow the journey they take through their social media activity, through to reading their emails, through to searching online.

Make the necessary changes

Your data analysis should give you a sense of what you want your website to be. You can then make the appropriate changes to your website to achieve these goals. Perhaps this is causing more specific call-to-action links. Or, maybe, it is writing longer descriptions under each product to make its purpose clearer.

No matter how big or small the changes are, they will be effective as they are directly correlated with what customers listed as their pain points. Rather than blindly making changes in the hopes that they will improve customer experiences, you can feel confident that they will. And, with the help of your visualised customer journey map, you can ensure that those needs and pain points are always addressed.

Your map should be a constant work-in-progress. Reviewing it monthly or quarterly will help you identify gaps and opportunities for streamlining your customer journey further. Use your data analytics along with customer feedback to check for any roadblocks.

I find it useful to keep all stakeholders involved in this process, so my maps are usually visualised on Google Sheets and shared amongst the people I work with closely. It is also beneficial to have regular meetings (quarterly or yearly) to analyse how new products or offerings might have changed the customer journey.

Customer experience

If I were to ask you when the last time was you had a really great experience as a customer, it probably wouldn't take you long to come up with the story of how the lasting impression of the experience made you happy and satisfied.

And the same goes for a poor customer experience, too – you could probably think of the story and reason within seconds and how the feeling afterwards was just the opposite. You probably felt angry, upset, annoyed, frustrated, or any combination of these negative emotions.

A positive customer experience not only results in making your customer happy, but it can also lead to additional revenue. The best marketing money can buy a customer who will promote your business – because they will refer their friends and family to you, free of charge.

The way you think about customer experience has probably had a profound impact on how you look at your business.

This is just one reason why creating and obsessing over a great customer experience is so important. And if the customer experience you have created is not great, you need to consider how to improve it and where to start.

Before we differentiate a good or bad customer experience, or for that matter, how to improve it, we first need to understand what customer experience is.

What is the customer experience?

The best way to define customer experience is the impression you leave with your customer, resulting in how they think of your brand across every stage of the customer journey. Multiple touchpoints factor into the customer experience, and these touchpoints occur on a cross-functional basis.

The two primary touchpoints that create the customer experience are people and product. Are you blown away by the performance of the product? Are you delighted by the attention a customer support rep gives you to help solve your problem? These are some general examples of what factors are at play when creating a great customer experience.

Since multiple teams impact the customer experience, let us break down how to measure performance to see if you are on the right track.

Importance of Customer Experience

Customer experience is of critical importance to the sustained growth of a business. It's important to ensure a positive customer experience, so customers build brand loyalty and affinity, evangelise about your product or service and refer their friends, and leave you positive customer reviews that will help your business retain revenue and earn new customers.

These days, the customer matters more than ever before. Customers have the power, not the sellers. Who gave them this power? Us. With help from the World Wide Web. Customers have more options than ever (your competitors), greater ease of switching power than ever (with so many subscription and freemium options), and more able to influence your business than ever (using social media and online reviews).

But it is a change for the best. Customers are your best resource for positively growing your brand awareness – because their recommendations shared with friends and family are more reliable than your marketing and advertising channels.

We have spoken about how important the customer experience is: How the customer feels about your brand. So, ask yourself, what happened the last time you had either a great or terrible customer experience? You probably went to a friend or co-worker to tell them the story, or you went to your social networking channels to broadcast your feelings to the world.

As a company, you must take this personally and obsess over why people feel the way they do about you – it will dramatically help you grow your business.

How to Measure Customer Experience

There are several ways to measure customer experience. Here are just a few.

Analyse customer satisfaction survey results

Using customer satisfaction surveys regularly or after meaningful moments along the customer journey will give you an idea of your customers' experience with your product or service.

A great way to measure customer experience is Net Promoter Score or NPS. This estimates how likely your customers are to promote you to their friends, family, and colleagues, determined by the experience you provide.

When measuring NPS, be sure to consider data in aggregate across teams. Since multiple teams impact the customer experience, we need a clear picture of performance and numerous data points. What is the NPS for in-product usage? What is the NPS for customer service teams across communication channels (phone, email, chat, etc.)? What is the NPS for sales? What is the NPS for attending a marketing webinar?

Multiple data points must be considered to determine the NPS of the overall customer experience. Your customers probably want to share their feedback, so let them. Analysing NPS from multiple touchpoints across the customer journey will tell you what you need to improve, where you are excellent, and which customers you can connect with and engage in advocacy and evangelism.

It is easy to skew NPS results, so be true to the data and take it personally when you see what your customers think of you. If the results show a poor customer experience, be open to making changes. If the results show a great customer experience, dive deeply into team-by-team performance to ensure you are meeting standards across the board. And make sure you are following up on customer feedback – whether it is positive or negative. Connecting with customers can deepen your relationship and improve your customer retention and loyalty outcomes.

Identify the rate and reasons for customer churn

Sadly, much as we would love our customers to stay with us forever, that is simply unrealistic, and we will have a natural 'churn' of customers. The first thing to do is to accept that it happens. Then quickly move to monitoring it and determining if this can be reduced. It is important that you learn from churn when it happens to (hopefully) prevent it from happening for the same avoidable reasons.

Make sure you're doing regular analysis of your churned customers, so you're identifying if churn rate is increasing or decreasing, the reasons why the customers churned, and what action your team could take in the future to prevent a similar customer from walking out the door.

Ask customers for product or feature requests

Create a forum for your customers to request new products or features to make your offerings more useful and helpful for the problems they are trying to solve. Whether that forum is an email survey, on social media, or on a community forum, allow customers to offer suggestions proactively. This does not mean you must implement all the customers' requests. But if recurring trends are cropping up again and again, they might be worth digging into with some additional research to see if they would be worth investing some R&D.

Analyse customer support ticket trends

Another regular practice to ensure you have created a positive customer experience is to dig into the tickets your customer support team is tackling every day. If there are recurring issues that cause much pain for your customers over an extended period, make an effort to try to resolve them – either with clearer in-app or product instructions, explainer videos or articles, or product tweaks to make the process easier.

How to Make a Great Customer Experience

To make a great customer experience, you need to: build a customer journey map and buyer personas so you can effectively understand and solve their challenges, build a positive connection with your customers, ask for and act on feedback from customers and employees on how to improve, create helpful educational content, and build communities for your audience.

As we have discussed, there are various touchpoints in the customer experience, so the first action required to improve the customer experience is to identify which touchpoint to start with. This will vary by industry and business, and you must identify, locate then improve these key touchpoints to make a significant difference.

For businesses with customer service teams that take incoming calls, think about reducing the customer hold time or service agent quota to ensure your customer service teams have the resources they need to provide a high-quality experience.

10 Ways to Improve Your Customer Experience Delivery

Want to improve your own customer experience delivery in a hurry? Here are ten things you can change today that will make an immediate impact on your customer interactions.

1. Be patient.

As they say, patience is a virtue — and it is one that people who deal with customers must have in buckets. Here are some tips for dipping into your inner well of patience when dealing with a demanding customer (or other work frustrations):

Take a deep breath and let it out slowly – If you are dealing with a customer on the phone, ask them to hold for just one moment. Then consciously focus on relaxing your body. If you are dealing with a customer face-to-face, remove yourself from their presence for a moment.

Slow down your speech – Sometimes, by acting patient, you can feel patient. Try to remember that it is not personal. The customer is not mad at you — at least, they should not be.

2. Really listen.

It simply is not possible to truly help a customer if you do not listen to their needs. Moreover, customers know when you are not listening to them, and their frustration level rises accordingly.

Listening requires more than just hearing. To listen, you must focus on what another person is saying. That means staying quiet and working hard to understand the message behind the other person's words.

3. Know your stuff.

You may have a winning smile, a personality without peer, and an uncanny ability to connect with customers. But if you are not an expert on your company's product or service, you are of absolutely no help to a customer who needs expertise.

Make it your mission to know your product and service line inside and out, so you will be able to answer just about any question a customer throws at you. Knowing your stuff enables you to move quickly, make the right decisions, and find workable solutions for your customers.

4. Show a yearn to learn.

Yes, you should strive to become an expert in your area. But you will quickly find that the more you know about your area of expertise, the more there is to learn.

You must own your personal learning and development. Do not wait for someone else to identify what you need to know. Seek feedback from lots of different sources on how to improve and develop. When training is offered, participate fully. Finally, integrate and apply what you learn into your everyday existing work style and flow.

5. Be proactive.

If you are looking to provide a great experience, you cannot be passive. You must take charge and control the experience the customer is going to receive. You must be proactive.

As soon as you understand a customer's problem, work to offer a solution. If others need to be involved in the solution-making, reach out to them quickly. Gather all relevant information from whatever sources are available. Ideally, you will be able to solve the customer's problem right away. If you cannot, tell the customer exactly how long it will be before you can, and then deliver on that timeline.

As you are working to solve the problem, be decisive. Your ability to be decisive stems from your understanding of the nuances of your business. Do not wait longer than is necessary to develop a plan of resolution and execute it.

6.   Follow-through.

If you tell a customer you are going to do something, do it. Keep your word. Your promise is a commitment. And if you do not have an answer just yet, let them know - Bad news is better than no news!

7.   Persevere.

Look, dealing with customers can be challenging. No matter how patient, proactive, or engaging you are, every so often, somebody is just going to let you have it. Fairly or not, they are going to direct all their pent-up anger and frustration at you. That is where perseverance comes in.

Letting all those negative emotions roll off like water off a duck's back is not easy but let them you must. You simply cannot permit yourself to wallow in the negativity. You must pick yourself up, dust yourself off, and let it go.

8.   Be fast on your feet.

Those who interact with customers regularly must be fast on their feet. That is, they must be able to triage a situation without really thinking.

To help yourself prepare for this, establish a set of triage guidelines. Do this before you are confronted with an unhappy customer. In these guidelines, include the name of your go-to person (or people) —that is, the person you will contact when you do not know what to do.

Be sure to have their contact info handy. Also, decide what information you will send up the chain of command if you are confronted with a customer challenge above your pay grade. Will you need to pass on verbatim recordings of an interaction? Will you need to share the customer's purchase history with the company? Whatever it is, try to be ready to communicate the whole story.

9. Smile.

Like yawning, smiling is contagious. Unless you are super creepy, when you smile at somebody, that person will probably smile back. A sincere smile works wonders! If you can keep smiling even when everything around you appears to be going south, you will find that others will smile too.

10. Manage your body language.

When it comes to how people perceive you, nonverbal communication — that is, body language — is hugely influential.

Here are a few points to keep in mind:

- ✓ Do not shield your body.
- ✓ Keep your hands away from your face.
- ✓ Do not fake-smile.
- ✓ Watch where you stand; give the customer personal space.
- ✓ Keep your hands out of your pockets.
- ✓ Do not fidget.
- ✓ Stand up straight.
- ✓ Face the person you are talking to.
- ✓ Stand still.

Benchmark your business against the rest of your industry.

No one needs to tell you that a great customer experience is critical to a company's success. But the other companies that are courting your customers? They know this too, and customers will gladly follow whoever serves them best. There is more pressure than ever on customer service teams to deliver an exceptional experience and keep up with–and even pioneer–industry best practices.

One essential way to maintain a competitive edge is by regularly benchmarking your performance against competing organisations in your industry, especially those you admire.

Benchmarking helps you view your performance and processes objectively as a customer would see you. Quantifying the gap between where you are now and the industries best enables you to set more meaningful goals and motivates your team to work towards the highest standard.

Here are several ways customer service benchmarking put teams on the path to doing their best work:

Discover areas that need improvement.

Seeing your metrics or processes side by side with other companies in your industry may open your eyes to weaknesses you did not know you had. For example, your time-to-close rate may be getting faster each month, but it could also be where you are falling furthest behind your peers. Or you might find you are one of the only organisations of your size that does not offer phone support, and that is affecting customer satisfaction. Once it is clear where your team has the most opportunity to improve, it is easier to determine where to focus your time and energy.

Pinpoint opportunities to reduce costs.

When you consider that billions of pounds are lost worldwide each year due to bad customer service, the costs of running a customer service operation seem validated. Nevertheless, the more efficient your operations, the more time is freed up for customers. Benchmark metrics in relation to overall revenue can shine a light on where your team spends above, below, or in line with other companies of your size. These insights can lead you toward better allocating the team's resources.

Grade performance objectively.

Customer surveys and operational metrics can tell you a lot about your customer service's health, but it is easy to get stuck thinking in a bubble. Benchmarking pushes you to grade yourself relative to other companies like you instead of simply past performance. Holding your organisation up to the industry standard keeps the focus on being the best among many, not just the company's best version of itself.

Gauge the success of your improvement initiatives.

We all know that feeling of finishing a multi-month, give-it-your-all project only to be asked, *"Can you point to a number that shows this moved the needle?"* Benchmarking quantifies the status quo and defines a jumping-off point that all improvement initiatives can be measured against. This way, in a few months' time, you can see if newly implemented processes or practices are moving the team closer to their goal.

Gain insight into the industry and universal best practices.

How you define success will undoubtedly be different from companies in other industries or even your competitors. However, it is helpful to know what other companies are doing, especially those setting the standard. To keep their customers happy and operations running smoothly. Other companies' successes and mistakes provide opportunities to learn and accelerate improvement and can open people's minds to new ways of working.

Service & Delivery: Conclusion

Customer service is simply not good enough if we are looking to SCALE our business. Everyone provides 'service' and whilst some get it right; many get it completely wrong. To get ahead in such a competitive market these days, there is a need to move from reactive to proactive and create a customer experience like no other.

Being proactive and giving due consideration to every opportunity to deliver an exceptional experience that will last long after the interaction is key to building a reliable team of avid fans of who you are and what you do.

That doesn't mean having a customer service department but ensuring every team member understands that every decision you make, every conversation you have, every interaction and intervention is an opportunity to WOW your customers, your prospects, and the public at large.

> *"If you can sell someone on an emotion,*
> *they will buy anything."*
> **Steve Jobbs**

And so get out of the perception that customer service is provided as and when required. Still, it is an experience that everyone in the team and everyone who hears, sees, and feels who you are and what you do, is emotionally moved by that experience.

Further reading:

There are some fabulous other reads if you would like to learn more about this. They include:

Fish *- A Remarkable Way to Boost Morale and Improve Results (Stephen C. Lundin, Harry Paul, John Christensen, Kenneth H. Blanchard)*

Raving Fans *- A Revolutionary Approach to Customer Service – (Kenneth H. Blanchard)*

Fans Not Customers *- How to create growth companies in a no-growth world - (Vernon W Hill)*

Chapter Eight:

Winning Team

Rome was not built in a day, and neither was nor shall be your business. However, Rome wasn't built by a single person either, but by a significant team of skilled workers, all dedicated to achieving a goal far more significant than any could have hoped to accomplish on their own.

To achieve significant and sustainable scale within your business, it is imperative to recruit, retain and reward a winning team.

> *"Until you have an employee,*
> *you are one."*
> **Napoleon Hill**

A BIG business with a SMALL team

I would love to say the quote is mine, but it is not. It has been taken (with permission) from one of my **#ADDAZERO** Explorer Clients during a mastermind session whilst talking about my frustration with the term 'small business'!

During mastermind, we discussed the speed of growth within his business and the need to recruit more new staff. He shared frustration regarding the limited number of highly qualified and experienced people within his currently available profession and seeking new employment.

> *Why are you only seeking those currently available,*
> *and not headhunting the best in the industry?*

I asked. And this led to the mastermind openly and quite vigorously discussing their perception of working in a 'small' business instead of one of the FTSE 250 companies.

One reported: *"I can't afford to pay the same as the city."*

"Why is that a problem?" I asked.

Reminding them of research into the 'Top 100 places in the world to work' (Forbes, 2000) and how more than 17,000 employees were surveyed. One of the questions being why they had voted their place of work as one of the best in the world, only to learn their salary came 11th on their list of priorities!

"Why would they leave a city job to work for us?" another asked.

"For the very same reason as you chose to leave the city and set it up in the first place," I replied!

You see, the FIRST and most fundamental problem with being a SMALL business is the word SMALL.

I do not care in what circumstances you find yourself.

I've yet to discover a positive use of the word SMALL when it comes to business! I am not sure how many people are excited by the word SMALL or would want to leave a BIG company with a BIG salary to take on a SMALL role in a SMALL company!

Even though my businesses have been members of the Federation of Small Businesses for well over 13 years now, I've forever challenged them to change their title to the Federation of Growing Businesses!

I recall a quote from none other than Warren Buffett, delivered during lunch to mark his 74th successful business launch. There were a thousand people in the audience that day, including press and reporters from all the major papers and news channels, all clambering to get a good shot and a quote from a man widely regarded as one of the most successful businessmen in the world.

> *"Most business owners think small...*
> *whereas I think BIG,*
> *and that automatically gives me the advantage."*
> **Warren Buffett**

And there it was. PURE GOLD handed to them on a plate. Most business owners are thinking SMALL. *Will I be able to? What if? When I can?* They think immediate and small, hoping they have sufficient to get by. They have a limiting beliefs mindset.

Whereas, Warren thinks in an abundance mindset. He has already determined the business's long-term goals and aspirations, possibly years and years ahead of the RIGHT NOW. And spends his time establishing HOW to achieve that with his new fledgeling business!

I am not sure exactly how many times I have coached business owners by stating, *"Start with the end in mind."* – However, you can probably guess it is a lot given the number of times I've mentioned it in this book!

Establish the answer to 4 questions, and only then can you begin on making *'the end'* a reality!

1. On what day are you going to sell the business successfully?
2. How much will you sell it for?
3. Who will you sell it to?

And the most challenging question for most to answer:

4. Why would they pay that for it?

For example: I help business owners change their perception of who they and their businesses are. Where they are, and where they are heading. And then provide the help, guidance, and accountability in order to achieve it.

A FUTURE organisational structure chart should be based 12, 24, maybe 36 months into the future. (Once you have completed ALL aspects of the #ADDAZERO Business Challenge, for example). Only once you (and your team) can easily visualise what the successful business will look like in the future can you begin to make that a reality! However, with so much to do and so little time, it is often somewhat difficult to know where to start!

So, whilst this is not a definitive chart, here is one we created for you as an example. To help you both understand how to achieve this, whilst also sharing our beliefs on the first nine roles you should consider within your growing business!

You will note, I have said ROLES and not EMPLOYEE's. Because it may be that you determine the need for several Employee's to cover some of the roles, prior to moving to the next. (3 x Production Operative, prior to taking on a Marketing Assistant)

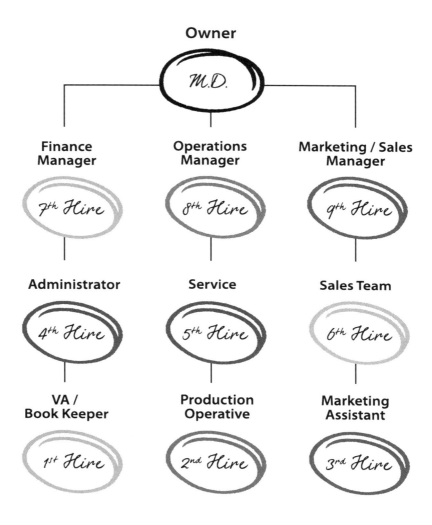

Here we have determined the model that has worked best within our own business and recognise it as the key elements of a growing business.

The next question is...

Where to start?

Before you begin writing the job advert, you need to determine what each of these positions shall be responsible for within the business and create a role contract (not a job description) for each.

A role-specific contract not only helps create buy-in by whomever you choose to offer the role to, but it also creates a greater sense of accountability to them and defines their contribution to the business.

This does not need to be reams and reams of paper, but should cover:

- ✓ **WHY**: The purpose of the role and how it fits with the broader business vision & mission
- ✓ **WHAT**: The duties to be performed, the results to be delivered, how the results will be measured. Including the conditions under which they are to be performed.
- ✓ **HOW**: The attitudes, behaviours and skills expected from the holder of the position

Next, it is time to systemise.

Working ON the role rather than simply IN the role can be crucial in documenting what the role entails. The Key Performance Indicators required to ensure it remains effective and will help determine the DISC profile as to who would be most suited to do this.

Now we know WHO is best suited to the role; let us find them! But who to hire?

Start in the bottom left of the table, and source your bookkeeper first! Once they are in position, move from left to right, and get your production assistant and marketing assistant next. Now move up a level and start from left to right again! It may be that you determine you need more than one production operative, and that is fine; keep recruiting what you need as you need it. These are more the format for role recruitment rather than specifically the first nine hires!

Maintain this hiring strategy until you have at least one person in each of the nine roles. Now you have a sustainable team on which you can begin to SCALE!

> **Point to note**: *DO NOT forget that throughout your entire recruitment/selection process, EVERY member of the team needs to buy into the Vision and Values of the company fully and acknowledge the importance **everyone** on the team plays in achieving that.*

Team Culture

We have already spent some considerable time talking about culture much earlier in the book. But here, we are also expanding. To look at **how** different people within the team contribute to the overall culture and 'tone' of the business.

What is 'team culture'?

By the most basic definition, team culture is made up of the values, beliefs, attitudes, and behaviours shared by a team. It is how people work together towards a common goal and how they treat each other. These attributes could be positive or negative.

Culture is a difficult concept to grasp because it is generally unspoken and unwritten. It is about the dynamics between humans. Different teams within a company can manifest their own culture. But they are typically influenced by the company culture.

What is a *'good'* culture, and why is it important?

Many companies will use the word 'culture' as a buzzword to attract talent. The following has been said far too many times:

> *We've got a great culture here.*
> *We have a ping pong table AND bean bags.*

Culture is created by people, not the objects placed around them. This is something I stress to people all the time. Putting a ping pong table on the floor of a corporate office made up of people with individualist or sexist attitudes will not automatically create a good culture. Culture takes time to build. It is not tangible.

Ping Pong Table ≠ Culture

A good culture is when team members collaborate, share knowledge, communicate, and most importantly, support one another. When people feel supported and know that someone has their back, they can do great things. It is like having a safety net that allows you to ask questions, have confidence, speak up and take on a challenge. Not only does this benefit the company, but it also supports personal growth.

In organisations (or even in a society) where culture is weak, you need an abundance of heavy, precise rules and processes. It leads to a permission seeking-based culture. When a culture is strong, trust exists, and people will do the right thing, thus creating an autonomous environment.

Strong culture = Trust = Autonomy + Efficiency

If you break a good culture, you break the well-oiled machine that creates your products. This broken culture can be reflected in the product/service, which determined the company becomes disjointed, broken and misguided.

Toxic Cultures

A company's culture begins from the values, behaviours, and decisions of an organisation's leader. If leaders act inappropriately and let unacceptable actions slide without discipline, this begins to normalise such behaviours as they trickle down through the management levels. The business culture changes very quickly, and it is so much more challenging to adapt a better culture than it is to destroy one!

What does cultural fit mean, and why is it important

Cultural fit is the ability for an employee to work comfortably in an environment aligned with their own beliefs, values, and needs.

When you are a cultural fit, you are more likely to enjoy your workplace, be happier, commit long-term, and be more productive and engaged. This benefits you and the company. It is a two-way street.

Cultural fit =
(Happiness + Productivity + Commitment + Engagement)

People are different: age, race, gender, perspectives, weaknesses. We need this diversity in teams as each experience will strengthen and add value to the team.

Cultural Fit =
Hiring people with the same personality as you

When hiring for a good cultural fit, it is vital to be aware of your own cognitive biases. It is human nature to gravitate towards like-minded people with the same personality or beliefs as your own.

In a situation where the culture is toxic, hiring in this way may further proliferate those undesirable traits, especially if it is coming from the top of the organisation, downwards.

***Toxic culture + Hiring based on same biases =
Further manifestation of the same toxic culture***

How do you *build* a strong team culture?

It is possible to grow and evolve a team's culture over time. It all starts with honestly identifying where you are now and where you want to be. The only way to make a change is to take ownership and action it as a united team. This is a lot easier when you have a good leader.

I believe much of this happens within the first 100 days! The 'clock' starts ticking from the moment someone sees the role advertises and submits either a resume or covering letter, or in some other way responds to register their interest. And from that moment forward, how the business responds to that begins to set their expectations and acknowledge **our** culture and values. By the end of a successful probationary period, much of the business's values and culture have already made an impression on the individual.

They will shape their relationship with the company. While it **is** possible to change this, it's far easier to step off on the right foot!

8 considerations when building a winning team

Shared vision

Share the long-term goals you have for your business with your team. Let them know what your vision is and what your plans are to turn this vision into reality. Explain to them where your business is heading in the coming months and where you see it going in the next few years. Once you have shown your team the big picture, it is time to zero in on the details. Help your employees understand how their roles contribute to your vision and how they fit into your plans.

Set team goals

Create shared objectives as a team that tie into your business goals. This helps your team know what they are working toward, their priorities, and how to make decisions that align with the team's shared objectives. These objectives also give your team a shared purpose, one that strengthens a sense of 'us' instead of 'them and me.'

Define clear roles and responsibilities

Make sure your team understands how their roles work together. Each team member's responsibilities are connected, and these dependencies are crucial to the team's success. For example, a person delivering late or failing to do something that's part of their job can cause conflicts and misunderstandings. To prevent this, discuss with the team how their roles are related and how each team member relies on the others for the entire team to do well.

Build relationships with your employees

Spend some time learning more about each member of your team – their skills, their strengths and weaknesses, their likes, and dislikes. Once you understand them better, you will know how to motivate them. You can match their skills to specific tasks and know which problems they can solve best. Get to know your employees outside of the workplace too. Ask them about their hobbies and interests. It's a personal touch that shows your employees that you care.

Show your employees that you value them

Recognise your team's efforts and reward them. Celebrate their successes – go out for a team lunch, give them a gift card or voucher for their favourite takeaway place, or feature them on your business website and social media accounts. Whatever it is, be genuine in showing your appreciation. Another way to motivate your team and keep them happy is to offer perks. This can be bonuses for excellent performance, new equipment, or a cool new uniform, or even shouldering the cost of training to improve their skills.

Embrace diversity

Each team member is different, and that can be a strength. Contrasting points of view help you find the best solution, so be open to other ideas and approaches. By embracing your team's differences, you are fostering creativity and innovation.

Be a good leader

An effective team needs an effective leader. Be firm yet approachable, fair, and true to your word, and treat each of your team members with respect. Leading a team may be new to you, so invest in yourself by taking training courses on leading and managing. It is a constant learning experience, and you will discover techniques that will work for you along the way.

Do fun team building activities

Doing activities together can help create shared experiences as a team and form good working relationships.

These activities build trust, improve communication, and help your team, work more effectively. Check your budget and see what you can afford. Team-building activities can be as simple as going out for drinks after work on a Friday night or even monthly game nights, movie nights, or quiz nights. Put some effort into it, and do not forget to relax, unwind, and enjoy.

Personal/professional profiling

We have already spoken at length about the benefits associated with you knowing and understanding your own psychometric profile. Team profiling provides an array of in-depth insights that can be utilised in various ways to make people work together more effectively.

What is team profiling?

Team profiling looks at what qualities each team member brings to the table and considers how all these individual qualities work together cohesively. A good team profile will identify strengths, find out where the team is most effective, and identify key development areas.

It helps the team understand and celebrate difference amongst its members and gives managers a real insight into what makes their team tick.

Questions to consider when team profiling.

- ✓ What does each person bring to the group that is special and different?
- ✓ Are tasks being done by the best people, and are there any gaps?
- ✓ How can I maximise motivation and performance?
- ✓ How can I interact successfully with each person?
- ✓ How do I manage the inevitable stresses and conflicts?

Profiling looks at what role individuals prefer to play in a team, why members feel motivated by some tasks and not others, and where individuals are most likely to focus their energy.

The benefits of team profiling

Profiling your team members can provide you with a variety of valuable insights that you can then consider when planning projects, structuring the team and recruiting new team members. It also provides valuable information of team members, and in a short space of time, team members can expect to:

- ✓ Understand how they can make the best contribution.
- ✓ Appreciate the need to work with others who operate differently.
- ✓ Optimise diverse strengths and get energies moving; and

244

✓ find it easier to communicate, resolve conflict and solve problems.

All the above will empower team members to work together more effectively and provide them with an insight into their colleagues, allowing them to adapt their approach to achieving the desired outcome.

There are various personality profiling tools available, such as DISC, Myers Briggs, and PROPHET, which will help you identify somebody's behaviours and personality traits during the recruitment process. You will then be able to match these against your requirements for the role and the team's existing profiles. Although these are a valuable tool in the recruitment process, please remember that they are only a guide and cannot be used in place of an interview. Often, your intuition can be more reliable than these tests!

DISC profiling is one of the more common forms of profiling and allows you to have a rating of an individual's attributes in the following areas:

✓ Dominance
✓ Influence
✓ Stability
✓ Compliance

This is a tool that I've used with my own teams, and through reverse questioning (answering the questions in the way that I'd like an employee to), I've been able to construct an "ideal" profile for particular roles.

Something to always bear in mind with these tools is that an individual's working conditions can influence them on a particular day – and indeed are possible to be manipulated.

There is also an "internal" DISC and an "external" DISC. In other words, the actual results and those projected to the outside world. In times of stress or pressure, an individual may revert to their "internal" DISC.

Organisational structure chart

As we have already mentioned, there are many benefits for having both a current and future organisational structure chart with every business.

You might argue that this is counterproductive for the time it takes to map it out until you have built a team. However, I cannot argue more strongly; this is not the case.

Remember, I have mentioned several times, you must know what the end game is and play it backwards. Therefore, in your 'future' business, will you NOT have a structure chart?

This makes hiring, role allocation, promotion, and such likes so much easier when you have already stopped considering WHAT the business requires before you are in the moment.

However, one of the biggest problems with recruiting talent at the top of their profession is convincing them that this business's role has progression opportunity. Why would anyone choose to give up a great career to come and work for a business with no future? They simply would not. Therefore, by having documented the future of the company, for everyone to be able to see clearly, where they currently sit "on the bus" (to coin Jim Collins phrase) and to where they could aspire to, is motivation that they are working for a progressive business with a future and career opportunities rather than a job!

Successful organisations strive to evaluate and guide their employees toward constant improvement, but a standard performance review system is often found wanting. While more and more companies are integrating a technique called 360-degree feedback into their review process, some are finding that it's not going as smooth and easy as they had hoped.

Organisations can do a poor job of introducing and using this type of multi-rate process. Still, it is possible, with the right steps, to do a good job of introducing and maximizing the value of 360-degree feedback. This matter's because nothing raises hackles as fiercely as a change in performance feedback methods, particularly when they may affect employee compensation decisions.

360-Degree Feedback

360-degree feedback is a method and a tool that provides each employee with the opportunity to receive performance feedback from his or her supervisor or manager and four to eight peers, reporting staff members, co-workers, and customers. Most 360-degree feedback tools are also responded to by everyone in a self-assessment.

360-degree feedback allows everyone to understand how their effectiveness as an employee, co-worker or staff member is viewed by others. The most effective 360-degree feedback processes provide feedback that is based on behaviours that other employees can see.

The feedback provides insight into the skills and behaviours desired within the organisation to accomplish the mission, vision, and goals and live the values. The feedback is firmly planted in behaviours needed to exceed customer expectations.

People who are chosen as raters, or feedback providers, are often selected in a shared process by both the organisation and the employee. These are people who generally interact routinely with the person who is receiving feedback.

The purpose of the 360-degree feedback is to help everyone understand their strengths and weaknesses and contribute insights into aspects of their work needing professional development.

Debates of all kinds are raging about how to:

- ✓ Select the feedback tool and process
- ✓ Choose the raters
- ✓ Use the feedback
- ✓ Review the feedback
- ✓ Manage and integrate the process into a more extensive performance management system

Looking at the pros and cons of this method can help with the decision-making process.

Pros and Cons of 360-Degree Feedback

Upsides

- ✓ Provides feedback to employees from a variety of sources
- ✓ Develops and strengthens teamwork and accountability
- ✓ Uncovers procedural issues that can hinder employee growth
- ✓ Reveals specific career development areas
- ✓ Reduces rater bias and discrimination tendencies
- ✓ Offers constructive feedback to improve employee outputs
- ✓ Supplies insight on training needs

Downsides

- ✓ Serves as only part of the overall performance measurement system
- ✓ Causes organisational issues if implemented in a hasty or incomplete fashion
- ✓ Can fail to add value if not effectively woven into existing performance plans
- ✓ Prevents recipients from getting more information because the process is anonymous
- ✓ Focuses on employee weaknesses and shortcomings instead of strengths
- ✓ Provides feedback from inexperienced raters, and groups can "game" the process

✓ Requires a large degree of data collection and processing in some cases

The Upside of 360-Degree Feedback

360-degree feedback has many positive aspects and many proponents.

It is a central part of many leadership development programs. It's also a practical way to get a large group of leaders in an organisation to be comfortable with receiving feedback from direct reports, peers, bosses, and other groups. Once leaders begin to see the enormous value to be gained, we see them add other groups to their raters, such as suppliers, customers, or those two levels below them in the organisation.

> *More than 85% of all the Fortune 500 companies*
> *use the 360-degree feedback process*
> *as a cornerstone of their overall*
> *leadership development process.*

Organisations that are happy with the 360-degree component of their performance management systems identify these positive features that manifest in a well-managed, well-integrated 360-degree feedback process.

Improved Feedback from more Sources

This method provides well-rounded feedback from peers, reporting staff, co-workers, and supervisors and can be a definite improvement over a single individual's feedback. 360 feedback can also save managers' time in that they can spend less energy providing feedback as more people participate in the process. Co-worker perception is important, and the process helps people understand how other employees view their work.

Team Development

This feedback approach helps team members learn to work more effectively together. (Teams know more about how team members are performing than their supervisor.) Multi-rater feedback makes team members more accountable to each other. As they share the knowledge that they will provide input on each members' performance. A well-planned process can improve communication and team development.

Personal and Organisational Performance Development
360-degree feedback is one of the best methods for understanding individual and organisational developmental needs in your organisation. You may discover what keeps employees from working successfully together and how your organisation's policies, procedures, and approaches affect employee success.

Responsibility for Career Development
For many reasons, organisations are no longer responsible for developing their employees' careers—if they ever were. While the bulk of the responsibility falls on the employee, employers are responsible for providing an environment in which employees were encouraged and supported in their growth needs. Multi-rater feedback can provide excellent information to an individual about what she needs to do to enhance their career.

Additionally, many employees feel 360-degree feedback is more accurate, more reflective of their performance, and more validating than feedback from a supervisor alone. This makes the information more beneficial for both career and personal development.

Reduced Discrimination Risk
When feedback comes from several individuals in various job functions, discrimination because of race, age, gender, and so forth is reduced. The "horns and halo" effect, in which a supervisor rates performance based on their most recent interactions with the employee, is minimised.

Improved Customer Service
Each person receives valuable feedback about the quality of his product or services, especially in feedback processes that involve the internal or external customer.

This feedback should enable the individual to improve the quality, reliability, promptness, and comprehensiveness of these products and services.

Training Needs Assessment
360-degree feedback provides comprehensive information about organisation training needs and allows planning for classes, cross-functional responsibilities, and cross-training.

A 360-degree feedback system does have a good side. However, 360-degree feedback also has a bad side—even an ugly side.

The Downside to 360 Degree Feedback

For every positive point made about 360-degree feedback systems, detractors can offer the downside. The downside is important because it gives you a road map of what to avoid when implementing a 360-feedback process.

The following are potential problems with 360-degree feedback processes and a recommended solution for each one.

Exceptional Expectations for the Process
360-degree feedback is not the same as a performance management system. It is merely a part of the feedback and development that a performance management system offers within an organisation. Additionally, proponents may lead participants to expect too much from this feedback system in their efforts to obtain organisational support for its implementation. Make sure that the 360 feedback is integrated into a complete performance management system.

Design Process Downfalls
Often, a 360-degree feedback process arrives as a recommendation from the HR department. Or driven in by an executive who learned about the process at a seminar or in a book. Just as an organisation implements any planned change, 360-degree feedback should follow effective change management guidelines.

A cross-section of the people who will have to live with and utilise the process should explore and develop your organisation's strategy.

Failure to Connect the Process
For a 360-feedback process to work, it must relate to the overall strategic aims of your organisation. If you have identified competencies or have comprehensive job descriptions, give people feedback on their performance of the expected competencies and job duties. The system will fail if it is an add-on rather than a supporter of your organisation's fundamental direction and requirements. It must function as a measure of the accomplishment of your organisation's big and long-term picture.

Insufficient Information
Since 360-degree feedback processes are usually anonymous, people receiving feedback have no recourse if they want to understand the feedback further. They have no one to ask for clarification about unclear comments or more information about ratings and their basis. Thus, developing 360 process coaches is important. Supervisors, HR staff people, interested managers, and others are taught to help people understand their feedback and trained to help people develop action plans based on the feedback.

Focus on Negatives and Weaknesses
At least one book, "*First Break All the Rules: What The World's Greatest Managers Do Differently*" (Coffman, 1999) advises that

great managers focus on employee strengths, not weaknesses. The authors said, "*People don't change that much. Do not waste time trying to put in what was left out. Try to draw out what was left. That is hard enough.*"

Rater Inexperience and Ineffectiveness

In addition to the insufficient training organisations providing both people receiving feedback and giving feedback, there are numerous ways raters go wrong.

They may inflate ratings to make an employee look good. They may deflate ratings to make an individual look bad. They may informally band together to make the system artificially inflate everyone's performance. Checks and balances must exist to prevent these pitfalls.

Paperwork/Computer Data Entry Overload

In traditional 360 evaluations, multi-rater feedback upped the sheer number of people participating in the process and the subsequent time invested. Fortunately, most multi-rater feedback systems now have online entry and reporting systems. This has almost eliminated this former downside.

360-degree feedback is a positive addition to your performance management system when implemented with care and training to enable people to serve customers better and develop their own careers.

However, if you approach it haphazardly just because everyone else is using it, 360 feedback could create a disaster requiring months and possibly years for you to recover.

There are negatives with the 360-degree feedback processes. Still, with any performance feedback process, it can increase positive, robust problem solving and provide you with a profoundly supportive, organisation-affirming method for promoting employee growth and development.

However, in the worst case, it saps morale, destroys motivation, and enables disenfranchised employees to go for the jugular or plot revenge scenarios against people who rated their performance less than perfect.

Which scenario will your organisation choose? It is all about the details. Think intensely before you move forward, learn from others' mistakes, and assess your organisation's readiness. Apply effective change management strategies for planning and implementation.

Do the right things right, and you will add a powerful tool to your performance management and enhancement toolkit.

Team: Conclusion

Behind every great business leader, is an exceptionally hard-working, loyal, and trusted team. You only have to watch any of the REAL winners at the many awards around the world. In every discipline, in every sector, as one receives the award, their speech always states they are receiving this on behalf of the team that has made it possible.

To grow beyond the ordinary, to achieve extraordinarily, we (both individually and as a team) must be extraordinary. That often means tearing up the 'rule' book and determining WHAT do we need to have in place to enable every member of the team at every opportunity to be the very best they can be.

Further reading:

There is one book, I've re-read time and time when it comes to team, and its: **Legacy**, by James Kerr.

You might also enjoy reading my first book **Battlefield2Boardroom** – 10 proven military tactics to combat Mediocrity

#ADDAZERO:

BaseCamp Conclusion

The guidance, advice, suggestions, and recommendations within this book are not to be taken lightly. My team and I have spent years researching, developing, testing, monitoring, reviewing, amending, and retesting every aspect of the advice within these pages prior to committing them to paper.

We worked with the business's owners during the BETA testing phase; ALL reported significant and sustainable growth BEYOND the business plan projections set prior to us working with them.

Businesses owners such as Richard:

I met Richard at a Regional Networking Event I had been invited to speak at with my keynote "Get BIG or Go Home". In January 2018, the network organiser felt a motivational keynote with a message about thinking BIG was a great way to start the year.

I was offered business cards from several the attendees and, as always, followed up with each one separately both with an email and telephone call.

Richard's call was significantly different from the rest of the calls made that day:

"Hello Richard, it's Jay from My TrueNORTH."

"I'm in," he stated. *"Tell me when you can come over and when we can start."*

I met with Richard shortly afterwards, and he explained that the content I shared within the keynote had already saved him around £600pcm and if I was able to do that for nothing, he wanted to know how much more we could do with some coaching.

Richard joined our #ADDAZERO Explorer Mastermind and has never looked back. We work with both him and the company's 'Number 2' as they apply the many teachings within these pages. We've supported the review of every aspect of themselves and their business offering, and made recommendations where efficiencies, automation or outsourcing can be made to support the business further. They have recruited three new senior hires and are currently increasing their back-office support team by five (since we began working together). Within the city where their head office resides, they are regarded as being amongst the best employers.

Within the first two quarters of applying this methodology, we had saved the business over £160K, and there is likely to be an ongoing saving of more than £50K per annum. Furthermore, we've helped Richard review and amend his plans for the future. With a new child recently born, now working with him to further systemise the business (the content of which is within the following book: #ADDAZERO – Scale & Exit) to reduce further the requirement for him to spend so many hours at work.

By supporting Richard to apply the many lessons within these pages, to ensure he has the right people, processes and systems within the business, they now have new national contracts with some of the biggest names in their industry and are working to win several others. And based on the Service & Delivery and Winning Team chapters particularly, the team have adopted this to an exceptional level of detail when it comes to customer experience. They are regularly being referred more work and recommended to some very elite industry-specific awards.

Richard has most recently been offered a lucrative offer to sell the business, but politely declined on the basis that "I'm having too much fun building it to think about what's next!"

And Catherine:

When invited by a fellow business coach, I met Catherine to present my keynote *"Get BIG or go home"* at one of his marketing mastermind groups.

After being made redundant and quickly moved from being a marketeer to the role of Managing Director of a Marketing Company, Catherine had formed her marketing agency. She was very similar to lots of other business start-ups and had been guilty of winning the work, doing the work, winning the work, and doing the work for a few years before joining the mastermind.

By her admission, she had joined a marketing mastermind group with hope to win clients from those, realising how difficult successfully marketing yourself can be, and used it as a networking/referral group more than to learn.

However, she realised from a conversation with me that the agency she had created required a lot more than simply good marketing. As an ex-employee had little knowledge or understanding of the other essential aspects of running and scaling a business.

After reading the book, and over the first 12 months, we helped Catherine with a business plan, a mission statement, and reviewing the agency's values and culture. She was stuck in an ambiguous, unfriendly contract with the landlord, which was causing stress and regularly taking attention away from the core of the business. By applying the teachings within this book, Catherine grew in both knowledge and confidence, sufficient to review and negotiate far better terms resulting in a 60% reduction in operating costs across the business.

Catherine also had a very junior and inexperienced team, which worked well whilst she was present, but less so whenever she was not. By applying the Customer Service and Winning Team lessons, she reviewed the terms of the contract to which they were employed. She also implemented some more demanding KPI's, carried out her first-ever employee annual review process and embarked on the subsequent dismissal and recruitment for replacement.

Almost as soon as she had completed the 'foundation' stages taught within these pages, Catherine announced she was getting married! After a prolonged engagement, a recent change in family circumstances resulted in Catherine choosing to marry, and together the couple announced their desire to travel extensively.

Catherine quickly found a buyer for the business for significantly more than even she had hoped to achieve. Her business's sale enabled her to take some much-wanted time out, enjoy a rather lavish wedding, and some extensive travel plans.

As Catherine retired from business to begin her "world tour", she was kind enough to remark that outside her marital relationship, she had enjoyed the affair of her life with the connection she made through following the programme detailed within the pages of this book!

And Mathew:

I was introduced to Mathew in early 2014. He is the founder of the practice operated from rented offices in the local city's suburbs, close to where he lived in Yorkshire. He had been trading for a few years, had a small but dedicated team of support within the business with great ambition to scale the company and the motivation to spend more time with his growing family.

I was introduced through a mutual friend when Mathew had approached him for some advice. He had been encouraged by '*colleagues* and *friends* down a particular path, despite his own better judgement. Sadly, he had eagerly been following some very poor advice, and on realising there was a significant 5 figure hole in his finances, had approached a trusted friend for an external viewpoint.

When we met, Mathew was very open and honest about his business. He quickly declared the current predicament, asking if there was an alternative pathway to grow the business or if he had done something wrong or overlooked something that had led him to the cash shortage he was currently facing.

We encouraged him to conduct our **#ADDAZERO** Foundations SCALE Audit, which revealed where the problems had occurred. He was then able to determine an action plan to change the business's direction and avert a cash flow crisis.

Although apprehensive about making such radical changes to how he operated the business, especially in the circumstances he was in when we met, Mathew had the courage and conviction to sufficiently trust the research and teachings to get started.

I still recall what he said as he first began to implement the many changes recommended based on the audit:

> *It's like standing completely naked!*
> *I have never experienced anything quite as deep,*
> *investigative and immediately actionable.*

Over the first few months of reading, considering, and implementing the teachings, we helped find a tax refund of nearly £35,000. His enthusiasm and determination to apply all the methodology was cemented! He continued to review and amend the systems and processes within his business sufficient for him to take on more staff, begin to branch out in terms of whom they did business with, what type of business and how much they charged.

Two years later, Mathew took his practice to London, opening offices in the city centre. He also bought a new building to house the head office big enough for the planned and progressive expansion and began trading internationally, eventually opening his first overseas office in Dubai.   Mathew currently employs three times as many staff as he did before being introduced to #ADDAZERO through Mastermind and has a business plan to support the role out into seven other countries over the next five years.

The simple fact is this works. However, only if you now put the book down! The teaching is now over (*for this book*). It is now time to IMPLEMENT!

YOUR BaseCamp Checklist

Here is a summary checklist to ensure you have grasped (and implemented) everything we have covered in this book:

MINDSET & MOTIVATION

1. You have had completed, and know your Psychometric Profile?
2. You dedicate a minimum of 30 mins EVERY DAY to PERSONAL Development?
3. You have absolute clarity on your PERSONAL and PROFESSIONAL 12-month goals?

VISION, VALUES, CULTURE, PURPOSE

1. Do you have a clear vision of your top 5 PERSONAL Goals?
2. Do you have a clear vision of your top 5 BUSINESS Goals?
3. Do you have an up-to-date, documented Business Growth Plan?
4. You have a healthy business CULTURE and a clear set of documented Company VALES to which all decisions are made?
5. You and your team CLEARLY understand your WHY?

STRATEGY & STRUCTURE

1. Have you identified your most Profitable/ Scaleable product/service?
2. Do you know your essential seven key business numbers?
   - 2.1. Number of leads
   - 2.2. Number of conversions
   - 2.3. Customer rention
   - 2.4. Average number value
   - 2.5. Fixed Costs
   - 2.6. Variable Costs
3. You review your Business Growth Plan at least weekly?
4. You Business Growth Plan is divided into 90-day chunks and sub-divided into weekly target
5. You have identified KEY TARGET AREAS for new customers to the business?

MARKETING MANAGEMENT

1. You have an exact marketing NICHE and have identified your ideal target customer AVATAR?
2. You have 'lead magnets' that are monitored, and are working effectively?
3. You have a CRM, with segmented lists and automation working effectively?

4. You have a good set of analytics on both your website and CRM, which is reviewed monthly?

5. You have a strong BRAND, which runs consistently through all your marketing ON and OFF line?

6. You publish a NEWSLETTER, giving added value to ALL of your lists?

MONEY & MARGINS

1. Do you have a robust Credit Control & Cash Collection procedure?

2. Do you have weekly Money Meetings?

3. You know, and monitor your monthly breakeven costs?

4. You get Monthly Management Account Reports, which you review and work to ?

SALES & NEGOTIATION

1. Do you have a clearly defined, profitable product/service?

2. Do you have a clearly defined Upsell/Cross-sell Strategy?

3. Do you have a sales system and script in place?

4. You have a documented Unique Selling Proposition which everyone within the team knows and refers?

SERVICE & DELIVERY

1. Have you mapped your customer journey?
2. You measure the delivery experience for every product/service to every customer?
3. You have benchmarked your business against everyone else in the industry?

TEAM

1. Your business and team are built upon mutually agreed upon Culture and Values?
2. Have you carried out Psychometric Profiling on your team?
3. You have an up to date organisational chart, based upon team profiles?
4. You host frequent 360^0 feedback meetings?

By implementing the recommendations within this book, you will already have begun to notice a marked difference in the way and manner in which you do business. By now, the People, Systems and Processes are beginning to work in unison to deliver a more sustainable scale model within your company.

But this is just the beginning!

Once you have implemented the guidance offered within this book, you will already have seen a massive shift in what you do, how you do, and its results.

Therefore, can you imagine what your business could look like when I share - **This is but the first third of the #ADDAZERO Methodology**?

You see, to build a significant and sustainable business, you must first build significant and sustainable foundations on which to build – BaseCamp.

Look out for the sequel to this book: #ADDAZERO – Scale to Summit (Due for publication Winter 2021), where I'll share the other two-thirds of the research, findings and methodology for you to hit the accelerator with confidence as we scale to success summit. You can keep informed of this and all other details of the **#ADDAZERO** Business Challenge by visiting the **#ADDAZERO** Website: *www.addazero.co.uk* and joining the newsletter mailing list.

Business Opportunity

Knowing what we do, regarding the success this methodlogy has for both businesses and business owners. We've made it our **mission** to support 1,000,000 Business Owners, **#ADDAZERO** to their Personal Disposable Income!

Why 1,000,000? - Well, when we first saw the impact it had on the BETA test group, there were approx 960K unemployed people in the UK! And, we know that during the course of implementing all that is within this book, the business **will** grow to a level you will require to increase the size of your team! (If nothing else, to free you up to enjoy life and all it has to offer, having generated so much more income)

Therefore, if we support 1,000,000 Business owners to scale, we can generate sufficient new jobs to eradicate unemployment in this country by creating more jobs than there are unemployed!

And, as members of the Global B1G1 programme, this meets several of the UN 17 Global Goals initiatives.

Whilst I'm dedicated to our mission, I acknowledge the need for a 'small army' of SCALE Sherpa's to provide the help, support, guidance, and accountability some business owners may require/desire to implement the #ADDAZERO methodology effectively.

Are you a Coach, Trainer, Consultant or Business Development Manager? Are you experienced in what **you** do, but perhaps don't have an end to end business growth mechanism to create real and lasting change for business owners and their businesses?

Visit www.addazero.co.uk website for further details about how you can train and qualify as a licensed **#ADDAZERO** Coach.

About Jay

Thank you for taking the first step to significant and sustainable growth for both you and your business. By doing so, you are already one step closer than all those who chose to pass this book by for something with a 'sexier' cover.

I'm Jay Allen. Initially trained in Sociology and Psychology (*with a particular interest in communication and human behaviour*) and then transferred to Emergency Medical Science to join the British Army as a Rapid Deployment Advanced Trauma Medic.

Throughout my 12+ years of service, be than on operational commitments or field exercises worldwide, I never gave up my interest in observing communication and human behaviour. Despite my career coming to an unforeseen and rather abrupt end - medically discharged – diagnosed with Post Traumatic Stress Disorder (2000).

I have subsequently used my education, qualifications, knowledge and experience to work at the most senior level for two of the largest high street stores and regionally within change management for the NHS.

I branched out to become a business owner in 2005, and since then, have either bought, acquired or set up from scratch four of my own businesses, successfully exiting twice.

Besides a love of research, I now busy myself speaking to business leaders worldwide on the **#ADDAZERO** Methodology and as the founder of My TrueNORTH – The UK's Leading Ethical Business Coaching Company.

Through this, we have made it our mission to help and support 1,000,000 Business Owners to significantly and sustainably grow both them and their businesses, with the ultimate aim to **#ADDAZERO** to their personal disposable income.

For further details about **#ADDAZERO**, to sign up to our newsletter, access the **#ADDAZERO** podcast, or **conduct your own #ADDAZERO Scale Audit** – Simply visit:

www.addazero.co.uk

Or, send an email to:

Iwantto@addazero.co.uk

Works Cited

Coffman, M. B. (1999). *First, Break all the rules.* New York City: Simon & Schuster.

Coleman, J. (2013, May 06). *Six components of culture.* Retrieved from Harvard Business Review: https://hbr.org/2013/05/six-components-of-culture

Collin / Porras, J. (1994). *Built to Last.* London: Radom House Business Books.

D.Ellis, C. (25 Jan 2013). *What it Takes: Seven Secrets of Success from the World's Greatest Professional Firms.* John Wiley & Sons.

Feinstein, A. (2014, April 8). *Why you should be writing down your goals.* Retrieved from Forbes: https://www.forbes.com/sites/ellevate/2014/04/08/why-you-should-be-writing-down-your-goals/#3b356c5c3397

Folkman, J. Z. (2014, November 24). *Why middle managers are so unhappy.* Retrieved from Harvard Business Review: https://hbr.org/2014/11/why-middle-managers-are-so-unhappy

Forbes. (2000, 04 01). *Best Companies to work for - 2020.* Retrieved from Forbes: https://fortune.com/best-companies/2020/search/

Gustavsson. (2018). *State of Health in the EU Cycle.* Paris: OECD Publishing.

Heskett, J. L. (8 Aug 2011). *The Culture Cycle: How to Shape the Unseen Force that Transforms Performance.* FT Press.

Hunt, S. (n.d.). *How to hire for culture fit, and why it matters.* Retrieved from Monster.com: https://hiring.monster.com/employer-resources/recruiting-strategies/workforce-planning/hire-for-the-organization/

Magretta, J. (2002, May). *Why business models matter.* Retrieved from Harvard Business Review: https://hbr.org/2002/05/why-business-models-matter

Osterwalder, A. (2004, January). *Business Model Ontology.* ResearchGate.

Porter, M. (1979). THE FIVE FORCES IS A FRAMEWORK FOR UNDERSTANDING THE COMPETITIVE FORCES AT WORK. *Harvard Business Review.*

Rogers, K. (2018, July/August). *Do your employee's feel respected.* Retrieved from Harvard Business Review: https://hbr.org/2018/07/do-your-employees-feel-respected

Wiersema, M. T. (1997). *The Disciplines of Market Leaders.* New York: Persues .

Printed in Great Britain
by Amazon